MOTHER THEKLA is Abbess of the Orthodox Monastery of the Assumption in Whitby, North Yorkshire. She is the author of *The Dark Glass* and co-author with the composer John Tavener of *Ikons*, both published by HarperCollins.

Forthcoming titles in the *Rhythm of Life* series

LIVING WITH CONTRADICTION
   – an introduction to Benedictine Spirituality
                                      Esther de Waal

TO LIVE IS TO PRAY
   – an introduction to Carmelite Spirituality
                                      Elizabeth Obbard

THE WAY OF ECSTASY
   – praying with St Teresa of Avila
                              Peter Tyler

R H Y T H M *of* L I F E
SERIES EDITOR : BISHOP GRAHAM CHADWICK

E T E R N I T Y N O W

An introduction to Orthodox Spirituality

M O T H E R T H E K L A

Foreword by JOHN TAVENER

CANTERBURY
PRESS
Norwich

First published 1997 by The Canterbury Press Norwich
(a publishing imprint of Hymns Ancient & Modern Limited,
a registered charity)
St Mary's Works, St Mary's Plain,
Norwich, Norfolk, NR3 3BH

British Library Cataloguing in Publication Data

A catalogue record for this book is available
from the British Library

ISBN 1-85311-161-9

*Typeset by David Gregson Associates, Beccles, Suffolk
and printed and bound in Great Britain by
The Lavenham Press, Suffolk*

Contents

Foreword

One thing I learnt very quickly from knowing and working with Mother Thekla is that she never compromises. And although she will change texts *ad nauseam* to fit my music, she will never change the initial meaning, the Orthodox meaning, which for her and now for me has become the only meaning. One could say that the whole force of Mother Thekla's work has been against the dreadful, appalling slimy morass of trivia that has bogged down our lives, the negation of all height and depth – the eternal platitude, the eternal commonplace, that is why Mother Thekla loves and often uses paradox, and the way of the 'intellectual fool', to turn everything upside down, so that we can forever *begin again*. She has often said that the narrower the path we tread, in the true Gospel sense, the more we are able to love and embrace other traditions. Not a mere social handshake, but at a much deeper level …. In other words, the closer we are to Tradition, the more we are able to 'see', until in eternity we will never have to 'see' again because we will be *inside* vision and Tradition.

This little book is not only for the Orthodox, but for all who seek truth, wholeness and fullness. Indeed, to all who seek 'the One who appeared among us like unto us … not in proud splendour and majesty, not as the avenger of wickedness, not as a Judge come to destroy some and reward others. No. He came with the gentle kiss of a brother …'*

JOHN TAVENER
Lefkandi, Evia, Greece
October 1996

*Gogol, *The Divine Liturgy of the Orthodox Church*.

vii

Series Introduction

Wisdom is to discern the true rhythm of things:
joy is to move, to dance to that rhythm.

These books on various traditions of Christian spirituality are intended as introductions for beginners on the journey of faith. They might help us discover a truer rhythm as something of the experience of those who follow any particular tradition resonates with our own.

Too much can be made of the distinctions between the different expressions of Christian spirituality. They all derive from the experience of what God has done and is doing in us and among us. While emphases differ, their validity is their congruence with the good news of Jesus Christ in the scriptures. As the various instruments in an orchestra make their special contribution to the symphony, so we delight in the extra dimension that each tradition brings to the living out of the Christian faith.

The present wide interest in spirituality seems to indicate that, in the midst of all the current uncertainties that we meet in contemporary life, despite its relative comfort and technological advance, there is felt a need to reconnect with our spiritual roots and find a deeper purpose for living.

Each volume offers an introduction to the essential elements of the particular spiritual tradition and practical guidance for shaping our everyday lives according to its teaching and wisdom. It is an exploration into the way that spiritual practice can affect our lifestyle, work, relationships, our view of creation, patterns of prayer and worship, and responsibilities in the wider world.

Many books, of course, have been written in all

of these areas and in each tradition classic commentaries are available which can never be surpassed. The aim of this series is to meet the needs of those searching for or beginning to explore the journey inward into their inmost being and outward to relationship with people and the whole of creation.

This volume introduces us to the Orthodox faith. Attending the Liturgy in the Russian Orthodox church on the Mount of Olives, with people moving from ikon to ikon, each representing one of the mysteries of our Lord, I felt an overwhelming sense of it all happening now, the birth, life, death, resurrection and ascension of Jesus, the coming of the Holy Spirit, all in the presence of the Mother of God and the Saints. Mother Thekla, in describing the feasts of the Orthodox Church, gives us a glimpse into the ethos of that tradition, the sense of 'the beyond in the midst', the eternal in the now.

BISHOP GRAHAM CHADWICK
Sarum College
October 1996

Preface

Orthodoxy is not a religion. The religion we all hold in common is Christianity. This is an axiom which, too often, is overlooked through sheer ignorance or, what is worse, prejudice.

Orthodoxy in England is a comparatively new phenomenon. Of course it can be argued that before the split of the eleventh century between the Roman West and the Orthodox East, everyone was 'Orthodox'. Some English converts to the Orthodox faith in fact are very busy seeking out early saints whom they feel permitted to venerate because they lived before that arbitrary and fatal date of 1054.

Many scholars have written about the unhappy split in the Universal Church, a split which grew gradually for the usual reason of greed for ecclesiastical power, but this is no place to discuss the evil misuse of dogma for political purposes.

As far as we are concerned, East and West 'split' – Western Catholicism gradually came under the power of the Patriarch of Rome (the Pope) and he spread his missionary work to cover all of what we now call Western Europe. Great Britain, with its Celtic tradition, held out against Roman sovereignty for some time. It is this Celtic tradition that English Orthodox are seeking to renew in their worship. In the meantime, Eastern Catholicism (Orthodoxy), initially rooted in the Byzantine Empire, spread throughout Eastern Europe. A thousand years after Christ it found its way to heathen Russia, there to become a traditional stronghold while Greece laboured under Ottoman rule.

Significantly, at the time of Russia's conversion to Orthodoxy, all the Church service books were immediately translated from the original Greek into

Slavonic, more or less parrot-wise – word for word, line by line – and these books exist to this day, in daily use, with some national peculiarities, but basically unchanged.

For Western Christians on the whole, Greek and Slavonic represent the Orthodox languages, but this of course is a simplification of ancient sources – Syriac and Arabic, to mention only two of the spiritual treasuries of the ancient world – and in modern times a variety of Eskimo languages, not to mention Japanese, American and Australian English. But, whatever the language, the sacred texts remain untouched.

Our texts are Orthodox. We are Orthodox. And from one end of the world to the other, in whatever language, we all pray the same texts from hour to hour, day to day, year in and year out. Dispersed as we are, all over the world, we keep our sense of unity not only in our liturgical texts but in our ecclesiastical allegiance.

Before Rome split from us, the Bishop of Rome (later the Pope) was one Bishop among the other bishops of the several Christian territories of the known world. After the split, the rest of us stayed more or less as we had always been but without Rome and her growing empire.

Traditionally, any Orthodox living outside an Orthodox country are looked after by the Patriarch of Constantinople, the Ecumenical Patriarch, senior amongst his equals. For example, the Archbishop in England, designated the Archbishop of Thyateira and Great Britain, is not in fact the Greek Archbishop, as many people suppose, but an outpost of the Ecumenical Patriarchate, intended to serve any Orthodox in England. In fact, the over-whelming majority of the faithful are Cypriot or Greek but there are plenty of others as well, not to be regarded as second-class citizens!

But whatever differences there may be of daily behaviour, of nationality, of language, whatever the local patriotism, we are all Orthodox. We may fight over calendars, or dislike each other's singing, or cling to our own habits of behaviour in worship, but, from one end of the world to the other, we can go into any Orthodox church, and whatever the language, whoever the Patriarch or Bishop, we know exactly where we are in the divine liturgy. Our Church is built on *one* Rock.

For the Orthodox, Orthodoxy remains the one and only living expression of their Christian religion, and, for us, it is *solely* the one expression: for others, it may be one of several. Ecumenism, where it touches our basic faith, is strictly avoided.

On the other hand, although we rigorously avoid ecumenism as it is practised, we firmly believe that if we believe in Christ, whether we are Catholic, Anglican or Protestant, or Orthodox, we are part of the body of Christ. And, if we accept the Creed as a doctrinal immutable basis to our faith, then we are not too far from each other, at least in the field of basic dogma.

In considering Orthodox *spirituality*, we can, I think, avoid direct debate on dogmatic differences, although, inevitably, dogma cannot but form the foundation, however hidden, for the explicit way of religious thought – of prayer, public or private.

It is my hope, however briefly and inadequately, to convey something of the essential fragrance of the Orthodox attitude within the common Christian tradition. What makes the Orthodox 'tick' differently from their fellow Christians (even if the inner mechanisms of their clocks are of the same metal and initial design)? What is there in our attitude which strikes an unfamiliar chime for those brought up in the Western tradition?

Chapter 1

Orthodox Essentials

It seems to me that the most individual aspect of Orthodox spirituality is the *objectivity*: a deep, resonant, grandfather note of indisputable reality. Our faith does not depend on personal motivation, personal reaction, personal pleasure or personal repugnance. Nor on personal *capacity*.

Our faith is ever *objective*, never *subjective*.

One day, we may wake up and feel nothing at all – no inner warmth; no inclination to prayer, but rather disinclination; a distaste for our parish priest; just dryness and emptiness. We may well experience discomfort, even agony of soul, a desperate spiritual boredom. But such a personal crisis has nothing to do with the objective faith: nor with the custodian of the faith: the Church: nor with the validity of the sacraments.

The truth does not depend in the least on the individual capacity for faith or worship. The Church, as one body, as the Communion of Saints, *believes*: it does not require or need in the slightest our personal belief to bolster it up – it is we who need our faith and the strength derived from the Church.

We go to church and attend the services of the Church not because we are 'good'. We go because we are bad. We need the health which only the Church can give us. Church services are not a reward. It is ever a privilege to enter a church and attend a service, never a duty or some form of benefit bestowed on the Almighty: church is both a form of spiritual hospital and the magnet of love, as Christ was in His life on earth.

Church services are not, on one level, for us, but rather an act of worship directed to God alone: it is for

1

us simply to stand and be drawn into the Communion of Saints, alive and dead, adoring God together with the angelic hosts.

The Prayers of the Hours

For Orthodox Christians the day is punctuated by the Prayers of the Hours – in churches, monasteries, and in some homes. Not everyone can say all the Hours, but between the whole body of the Church, little of the day or night is left without prayer.

At the opening of each Hour, we pray for the presence and forgiveness of the Holy Spirit. Without the Spirit we know that we shall remain paralysed and frigid. We beg for the warmth of the Spirit:

King of Heaven, Comforter, Spirit of truth, everywhere present and filling all things, treasure of blessings, and giver of life, come and abide in us, cleanse us from all corruption, and, of your goodness, save our souls.

The Divine Liturgy

In the Mystery of the Liturgy, the Priest leads us *away* from the world towards the reality beyond the present. The Priest faces the east – as a shepherd he leads his flock towards the light eternal – away from all that besets and bewilders us in our daily life. At other times it may well be a priestly duty to minister to our troubles, our sorrows, the manifold ills of the world. But, during the precious, and only too short time when the world, as it were, is re-directed to heaven, then he goes ahead of us into the light – away from the darkness of the world.

It is an objective call and we make an objective response. In the Divine Liturgy, we sing:

'Let us now lay aside all the cares of this life.'

Perhaps the key to the Orthodox tradition of worship is *objectivity*. How does such objectivity in the first place affect sacred art in its various forms?

Church Music

The music of the Orthodox Church is not personal: it is not composed according to individual taste or the climate of the times: instrumental accompaniment, such as that of the organ, is not permitted. The human voice is the medium of worship.

Orthodox church music derives from the Byzantine eight tones. I say 'derives' because, of course, over the centuries the introduction of some diversity is inevitable: the Russian eight tones no longer overtly resemble the Greek. Yet Orthodox national music, whether of Greek or Slavonic origin, remains constant to impersonal tones, sung by the person or persons of the appointed singer or singers.

Individual members of the congregation may occasionally join in when a particular melody is familiar and loved, but there is no question of 'organized' congregational singing nor of the worship being interrupted for instructions to be given to the congregation. Normally we stand throughout the services.

Texts

The sacred music is constant and so are the texts of the services – whether in the Greek or the Slavonic or in later translations.

No personal interpretations or interpolations intrude on the objective worship: the texts are as they were when they gradually evolved in the early centuries of Christianity. The Service Books have not been condensed or expanded – other than for the inclusion of more saints as the years of persecution went on. No saint has been excluded!

We pray what our fathers and forefathers prayed, even if we do not always understand fully the language in which we are praying. But this does not worry the indigenous Orthodox! It is the prayer that matters – not our enjoyment of the prayer.

At evening, as the sun is setting and the cares of the world begin to retreat for the night, and something of the peace not of this world penetrates from out the shadows, we sing the Vespers hymn – a hymn unchanged sung by the Orthodox over the centuries. Unfortunately, in translation, the original rhythm is lost but the meaning persists:

Glad light of the holy glory, of the deathless Father, heavenly, holy, blessed, Jesus Christ, we have come to the setting of the sun, and seeing the light of evening, we sing Father, Son, and Holy Spirit God. It is meet at all times that your praises be sung by the voices of the righteous, Son of God, Giver of Life: wherefore the world glorifies you.

Ikons

Hearken O Lord my God from your holy dwelling-place and from the throne of your glory in your kingdom and mercifully send down your holy blessing upon this Ikon and with the sprinkling of this sanctified water bless and sanctify it and give it the power of healing every sickness and infirmity, the power of driving off every crafty design of the devil from those who in faith seek refuge with it, and praying to it and seeking refuge with it worship you in front of it: and may their prayer ever be heard and pleasing to you.

What then of the ikons now becoming so popular in non-Orthodox circles both as objects of art and the cynosure of idiosyncratic prayer and devotion?

If we consider ikons not as something isolated, something outside the whole body of the faith, then, of course, there is nothing against every religious picture being referred to as an ikon, and treated as an *objet d'art* – or as the general property of at least

4

any Christian. But, if we see the Ikon within the whole body of Orthodox worship, an integral and vital organ, then the loose use of the term becomes nonsensical – if nothing worse – and idle admiration hardly the point.

An Ikon, as an *Ikon*, may not be divorced from the Orthodox faith as a whole, if for no other reason than that there are special prayers appointed by the Church for the blessing of Ikons by priests of the Church. These prayers are specific in dogma. 'Economy' (see Glossary), as ever in the Orthodox Church, allows for some exceptions to this general rule. If, for some reason, it is not possible to have an Ikon blessed according to the full ritual with all the prayers obtaining, it is permissible to have the Ikon within the Altar (the Sanctuary) for a certain length of time during which, as we say, 'it blesses itself'. Even so, it is preferable, whenever possible, to have the traditional sacramental blessing.

The prayers of blessing vary according to the dedication of the Ikon, whether to our Saviour Jesus Christ, his Mother, angels or saints. But the essence of the service is constant: the blessing which gives the Ikon the grace to be venerated. And, once blessed, an Ikon must be venerated – treated with meticulous respect. It is not a picture to be laid face down on the table. In the image of a lightning conductor, the Ikon may be seen as translating into the world that which is beyond.

For the Orthodox, the Ikon is in no way a decorative addition, not even a 'prayerful' one – it is *essential*: the focus of Christ's divine condescension in his Incarnation: a visual explication of the Creed.

He, who with his inexpressible concern before his willed Passion condescended to inscribe without the use of hands the image of his God-Man face on the handkerchief, Christ our true God, through the prayers of his most pure Mother and of all his Saints, will have mercy upon us and save us for he is good and he loves mankind.

The Ikons of the Theotokos show her with her Son. She is not alone. Her glory derives solely from him. Often the baby's face is wrinkled with age. The body is long and unchildlike. This is because for him there can be no time, he is ever man, and he is ever God.

The walls of our churches are covered with the Ikons of saints. It is an immense family, a formidable cloud of witnesses. Oil lamps and candles burn before them, they surround us from all sides, comforting, teaching, reproving, showing the way which they have trodden and which is, therefore, not impassable. We are not left only to read the lives of the saints in books, but we have them there in person within the Mystery of the Ikons, and it is a warm encounter.

The Ikonostatsis

This speaks of entrance and division.

The presence of the ikonostatsis, bearing its traditional ikons of Christ, his Mother, his fore-runner John the Baptist and the ikon for the dedication of the church, is a constant reminder of both division and unity. It speaks of the division between us and heaven, the division which we, as mortal men, cannot, and must not surpass. At the same time it speaks of the unity of the Incarnate God and the mediating saints. The officiating priest is the mediator, uniting us in spirit and in reality through Communion with Christ himself.

The altar is behind the closed doors of the ikonostatsis; with earthly eyes we cannot see the Transcendent. But, we are not left uncomforted. At Pascha, the doors are flung wide. Christ is with us — here on earth.

At other times we accept the humility of division and the Mystery. It is not for us to peer and pry and comment on the Holy Sacrament of the Eucharist. It is enough to be allowed to approach with unclean lips.

Candles

Once again we meet a question which may well be asked on a rational basis. What is the point of lighting candles either for ourselves or for those we love, the living and the dead? For the health of the living, or the peace of the dead in the company of the righteous?

Are the candles perhaps a gesture of self-indulgence? Something to satisfy our personal emotion? To some extent they may well be. And why not? After all, we are human beings with human emotions and what better place than before an Ikon to put our symbol of burning sacrifice?

Yet, at the same time, the offering of lighted candles is not merely some form of aesthetic satisfaction, or of ritual – or an effort to induce an atmosphere conducive to prayer. No, underlying the offering of the lighted candles is the foundation of Gospel Truth: our light must shine before men. It is not to remain hidden.

Our faint beam, on the wings of prayer, soars up to heaven, to the brilliance of Glory: the uncreated Light, which cannot be seen, but in his Love for mankind became visible. 'That was the true Light, which lighteth every man that cometh into the world.'

In lighting a candle, we offer up to him, the one *true* Light, in love and humility, our poor little lights, confident in the knowledge that in his infinite mercy, somehow, they will merge into the radiance of the Kingdom of Heaven.

And, on quite another level, candles express the plain, common-sense objectivity of faith – 'put a candle for me.' No analytical questioning can detract from this self-evident act of intercession within the Communion of Saints.

The Sign of the Cross

We make repetitive use of the sign of the Cross as for

us, it is both a protection and an assertion, a confirmation of our faith.

During the Service of the Liturgy, in particular, the sign of the cross is the practical manifestation of our participation and personal implication. *In the name of the Father, the Son, and the Holy Spirit* – three times we cross ourselves, acknowledging and confirming our faith in the Trinity.

Lord, have mercy, we plead before God, and so we cross ourselves to witness to our belief in the Trinity: Father – Son – Holy Spirit – One God – Three Persons – hence the placing of the fingers as we sign ourselves in witness of our faith – three fingers together for the Holy Trinity and two for Christ, Perfect God and Perfect Man.

Prayer, posture and movement invariably are the objective expression of our personal participation in the doctrine of the Church.

A word on fasting

For us fasting is not a penance.

Once again our practice is rooted in objective reality. Who would wish to sit down to a hearty meal or drink champagne when Christ is being crucified? As we feast – so we fast.

We prepare for every feast by fasting, as the wilderness precedes Pascha. Every Sunday we celebrate the Resurrection and we prepare for it by the fasts of Wednesday (the Betrayal) and Friday (the Crucifixion). In like manner we prepare for every great feast of the year.

The fasts are as real as the feasts. They ensure a spiritual as well as physical balance to the liturgical year. The human body and spirit would suffer from the monotony of constant feasting or constant fasting. Alternating feasts and fasts keep us spiritually alert.

8

Holy Communion

If Christ is to enter at Communion, how can we first fill our bellies with carnal food?

By way of the actual structure of the church, by way of the music, the ikons, the candles, the very stance of the faithful – 'stand upright', the Liturgy says – we come to the central focus of our Faith: Holy Communion. The body and blood of our Lord Jesus Christ is not a matter for equivocation or discussion, but a *fact*.

From the time that we are babies, through childhood, adolescence, youth and old age, our sins forgiven in Confession, we are admitted to the Mystery of Holy Communion.

Little children, as yet too young for Confession, are presented for Communion in their mothers' arms. They are none the less full members of the Church and approach as individuals: we make our Communion as *persons* before God. The celebrating Priest bestows the body and blood on each communicant by name: 'Servant of God, *Name*, receives … ' 'Handmaid of God, *Name*, receives …'

There can be no possibility of equivocation. The wine and bread *are* the Body and Blood of Christ. As we communicate we are given our names and thus confess individual responsibility of faith in the truth of the sacrament. The reality is incontrovertible reality. The warning is awesome and inescapable:

Not unto judgment nor unto condemnation be the partaking of your holy mysteries to me, O Lord, but unto the healing of soul and body.

Service Books

The Church calendar comprises fasts and feasts and 'ordinary' days of the Church year.

Such is the natural tenacity of the Orthodox attitude of faith that we have not found it necessary to amend, discard, or replace our texts for centuries. All that has happened, in the natural course of events, is the inclusion of new martyrs or other men and women remarkable for their holiness.

Not only are the texts unchanged but essentially they remain the same in the manifold languages of the Orthodox. After approximately a thousand years it is still possible to follow a Greek text, sometimes even word for word, in a parallel Slavonic text. There are, of course, a few minor differences but essentially the Books remain unchanged.

Whatever the slight variations in text or tone appointed for a specific hymn, the books themselves are common to all Orthodox.

There is the Book for each day of the week in eight tones, the Book for the Great Lent, the Book for Holy Week, the Book from Pascha to Pentecost – the twelve Books for the twelve months containing all the services for every saint, the Book of Psalms divided for recitation throughout the year, the Book of Hours and the *Typikon* for instruction as to how to combine the other books!

There is no opportunity for personal choice or devotion. The services are appointed. We may join in when and how we are able, in monasteries, churches or homes, but we can only join in, it is not for us to improvise or devise services to our own liking! Instead of asserting individual personality, we are invited, within the structure of the services, to merge into the unceasing worship of the mighty Communion of the faithful, here and in heaven.

The service books lead us into the celebration of the great feasts of the Church, the landmarks of our faith.

Feasts

It is surely in our feasts that an onlooker may find what is peculiar to Orthodox worship – the concept of immediate reality.

We do not simply *commemorate* the events of the Gospel, nor later events, they are not past events for us, a theological statement, but they remain for us an immediate experience. We celebrate the actual fact which we live and re-live each year as if for the very first time. It is not an act of meditation, but an actual *experience*, one which is immediate, urgent, absorbing.

On our feast days, it is as if we step out of the constriction imposed by finite time into a reality which is ever present: TODAY!

In the following chapters we may trace this spiritual journey through the words of our feasts. The liturgical year begins on 1 September and it is not long before we encounter our first Feast.

Chapter 2

Feasts of the Mother of God

It is not for us to discuss the Mother of God; there is nothing really to discuss. It is enough to know that she alone was chosen by God, Father, Son and Holy Spirit, to be the Mother of God Incarnate – Perfect God and Perfect Man.

Discussion about her 'place' in the realm of devotion is nonsensical: she has her inalienable place as *his* Mother. Surely we are left with nothing to do but approach her with loving veneration – the Mother of our God Incarnate.

Apart from all else, we are *grateful* to her for her obedience to the divine invitation. She could have refused to listen to the angelic message.

It seems appropriate therefore to start with her feasts and, it is revealing, that her feasts fall *before* Christ's birth and *after* his Ascension. During his life on earth, she remains subordinate, relative to him; hers is a loved place but ever emphatically non-divine – subordinate.

Again and again, in our worship, in the texts of the Services, it is made abundantly clear that we love and venerate the Mother of God for *his* sake – as the initial medium of our salvation.

The Nativity of the Mother of God (8 September)

Your birth, Mother of God, proclaimed joy to all the world: for from you rose the Sun of Righteousness, Christ our God: the curse he destroyed and blessing bestowed: and vanquishing death, he granted to us eternal life.

12

These are the words of the *Apolytikion*, the hymn of the day, sung in Tone IV, addressed to the Mother of God.

Immediately we meet the doctrine within the warm greeting. Her inalienable place is never separated from the fundamental *reason* for such a place. Through her, through her obedience to the Word, the Word could be made flesh and live among us.

At the very moment of the birth of the Mother of God, although as yet unrecognized and unproclaimed, joy has already entered the world: a hint of redemption. Birth pangs of the Fall, but, pangs to bring universal gladness, no longer the grief of Eve.

There is no place for extraneous notions, for pious commentary within the realism of the faith, hence, already at the moment of his Mother's birth, Christ's own birth, his Crucifixion, his Resurrection, are already contained in the few words of the hymn addressed to his Mother.

It is in the very essence of the Orthodox living theology that all is one; idiosyncratic devotion finds little place in the body of worship. All is part of one illimitable divine dispensation.

The theme is repeated in the second hymn of the Feast – the *Kontakion*:

> *Joachim and Anna were freed from the reproach of child-lessness, and Adam and Eve from corruption of death, in your holy birth, Most Pure: your people also celebrate this, delivered by it from punishment of sin, and they cry to you: the Barren has born the Mother of God and the nourishment of our life.*

But, as ever, the realism of the Orthodox faith has little time in its worship for any form of isolated concept. Its concern is with the event – the objective enacting of the *now*: timelessness and reality meet in a sphere beyond the comprehension of day-to-day logic. We plunge headlong into the actual celebration of the birth – the *now* of the joyous event.

13

If we join the crowd in church celebrating the Vigil of the Feast, we are led further into the event. The psalms are the customary ones, but verse after verse which accompany them reflect on the timelessness of worship:

Today God who rests upon the spiritual throne has made ready for himself a holy throne upon earth ...

The East Gate, newly born, awaits the entrance of the Great Priest. She alone brings into the world the one and only Christ, for the salvation of our souls ...

Today grace begins to bear its first fruits, making manifest to the world the Mother of God, through whom things on earth are joined with heaven, for the salvation of our souls.

Statement follows statement of the *fact* of redemption through the subsequent obedience of this scrap of humanity who was destined to become 'the only gateway of the Only-begotten Son of God'.

The Fall was real. The years of the Old Testament were real. And now:

Today is the beginning of joy for all the world; today the winds blow that bring tidings of salvation. The barrenness of our nature has been loosed ...

All is *real*. So too is the faith in divine providence and, so typical of Orthodox worship – the interweaving of Old and New Testament truth:

... for lo, she who was foreordained from generations of old as Mother and Virgin and Receiver of God, comes forth in birth from a barren woman: a flower has blossomed from Jesse, and from his root a branch has sprung. Let Adam our forefather be glad and let Eve rejoice with great joy.

The *fact* of the event commemorated is, as it were, hammered home: there is no theory – only event.

She who was preordained to be the Queen of all and habi-
tation of God, has come forth today from the barren womb
of joyful Anna. She is divine sanctuary of the eternal
Essence ...

There is an immediate sense of triumph over evil; at
the instant of birth, the whole history of our salvation
springs into action, *'for today is born of the seed of*
David the Mother of Life, who destroys the darkness.
She is the restoration of Adam and the recalling of
Eve ...'

This is no idealism, nor yet teaching, no parable, no
metaphor: *'She is the holy Temple ... wherein was*
accomplished the marvellous mystery of the ineffable
union of the natures which come together in Christ.'

During Matins, as the Canons are sung, the theme
not only remains unchanged, but is reiterated again
and again, more and more emphatically: the constant
theme of the reality of the Mother of God as a truly
natural infant; there is not the vestige of the possibility of error or any form of idealistic interpretation
which might lead to doctrinal error. She was born –
really born. And, what is more, our love for her cannot
be separated from her destination: it is hammered into
us during the service that her part in our salvation is
relative to the divine: she is destined to be the instrument, and only the instrument, of divine condescension in choosing to become incarnate:

You alone, O Sheep without blemish, from your womb have
offered to Christ, the Lamb of God, our substance to be his
fleece: therefore in our hymns we all honour you on this day
of your nativity from Anna.

Her *only* honour, great as it may be and is, lies in
permitting herself to be the birth-giver of Christ God.
Great as it is, it remains a relative honour, never
'competing' with the honour due to God alone:

Who has ever beheld a child whom no father begat reared
on his Mother's milk? Or where has a Virgin Mother ever

15

been seen? Truly, O pure Mother of God, in manner past understanding, you have fulfilled both these marvels.

Inevitably, we discern the objective continuity of divine history: no stage of the New Testament is isolated from the prophecy of the Old – nothing, as it were, hangs in mid-air, in isolation from the overall pattern:

The rod of Aaron is an image of this mystery, for when it budded it showed who should be priest. So in the Church, that once was barren, the wood of the Cross has now put forth flower, filling her with strength and steadfastness.

Once again, here is the reality of *worship*: not any abstract devotion, or evaluation of the Feast, but a time for active response to divine invitation:

Let us, the faithful, glorify the all-holy birth of the Mother of God in psalms and hymns: let us worship with faith the God who never lies, and who swore of old to David to give him a fruit of his loins ...

It is not for us to linger on the secondary, however beloved. Again and again, we revert to the basic reality of the faith: we return to the dynamic force, to Christ God. Even as we extol his Mother, we turn to him:

O you people, let us sing the praises of the Cause of all things, who caused himself to become like unto us ... let the children of Adam dance and sing. For the Rod is born, from whom as a flower sprang forth Christ, the only Deliverer of Adam.

Of course we love the Mother of God as a pure, self-effacing woman, a woman of the deepest spiritual obedience and courage. But her special place, wholly inalienable, is her unique reality as the Mother of God Incarnate. Already, at her birth, this one reason for our unfailing veneration is remorselessly hammered in – there must be no possible question of her place *vis à vis* God. The metaphorical language

16

dedicated to her is richly varied but ever constant in its analytical objectivity: we may love her – we do love her – for herself, but never by herself:

O Undefiled, we feast and venerate with faith your holy birth according to the promise: for thereby through Christ's appearance, we have been delivered from Adam's ancient curse.

Theology is expressed in the idiom of poetry:

You have loosed the unbreakable bonds of childlessness. You have given the barren woman a fertile offspring and a glorious fruit. Of that same offspring you have yourself become the Son and shoot: when you came to dwell among us, O merciful Lord, you chose her as your Mother according to the flesh.

Objective reality: as our worship, so our theology. Theology for us is not a theory, a rationally developed concept, an exposition of critical analysis; it is no subject for fundamental interrogation. For the heirs of the Renaissance, the Renaissance of the West which in its degraded form inevitably pointed the way to humanism, theology is childishly naive. For us, our theology is merely the exposition of the Divine Word. Hence the even primitive nature of the worship: we sing the truth, as we know it, of our faith:

We venerate your swaddling clothes, O Mother of God: we glorify the Lord who gave you as fruit to her that before was childless. He has opened by a miracle the barren womb of Anna: for, as Almighty God, he does whatsoever pleases him.

The epitome of the Feast as it were comes in the final doxology of the Lauds psalms. These words are sung in Tone VI, which is mainly reserved for the most solemn or mournful occasions:

This is the day of the Lord: rejoice, ye people. For, lo, the Bridal Chamber of the light, the Book of the Word of Life, has come forth from the womb, and the East Gate, newly born, awaits the entrance of the Great Priest. She alone brings into the world the one and only Christ, for the salvation of our souls.

Solemnity and mournfulness accompany the first step to our salvation. Her glory and her immeasurable grief are inseparable: a sword will also pierce her side, Simeon warned her: the infant born 'today'.

The Entry of the Mother of God into the Temple (21 November)

Let the gate of the temple wherein God dwells be opened: for Joachim brings within today in glory the Temple and Throne of the King of all, and he consecrates as an offering to God her whom the Lord has chosen to be his Mother.

The Law is being fulfilled, but as yet unwittingly: and in celebrating the Entry of the Mother of God we respect this 'overlapping'. We know who she was – we know she would fulfil the Law and thereby give us a new Law, but the parents of the Mother of God faithfully acted according to their faith and duty and we preserve the historic truth of this.

Our attitude is practical and the facts of a Feast remain facts; they are respected, praised and sung as facts.

It is important for the concept of continuity from Old to New not to be broken. Nothing is not clearly divinely ordained as from the beginning: all is fulfilment, never innovation. The real will of God is witnessed in the Scriptures: 'David prophesied concerning you, O undefiled, foretelling your entry and your consecration in the temple.'

As ever our reverence has an *objective* purpose. It is a theological devotion, however personal or even emotional it may appear in practice:

18

Zacharias rejoices as he receives you at your entry this day into the temple, Mother of the Word of life, who, Virgin before childbirth, have remained Virgin after childbirth.

Yet, together with the overt objective theology, there comes the warm, immediate gladness in the Feast. The Feast is being celebrated *today* – the sorrow of tomorrow is not to be anticipated at this time of gladness. Today we are glad because salvation is coming to us:

Let us, the faithful, dance for joy, singing to the Lord with psalms and hymns, venerating his hallowed Tabernacle, the living Ark, that contained the Word who cannot be contained.

How could we express the theological concept more concisely and precisely than in these few words? The image of the ark containing the precious objects of the Old Covenant now becomes the Womb of the Mother of the Incarnate God containing the young child destined to be the Mother of the Word, the New Covenant fulfilled in the Divine Person.

But, even more, the eternal divine paradox: she will contain what cannot be contained. She will conceive, without seed, the illimitable Person of God, Perfect Man.

It is all so vast, so wholly beyond our intellectual grasp and yet, it is so real. The simple veneration hardly makes any demand on us, but only asks the delight of participation in the Feast. Why need we be anxious at any feeling of bewilderment we may experience? The angels of heaven themselves are puzzled.

All the powers of heaven stood amazed, seeing the Holy Spirit dwell in you ...'

Above all else, again and again, we are forced to remember the *reality* of the event. We are never permitted to make any faint-hearted figurative approach; there is nothing metaphorical here:

19

> *Today the Mother of God, the Temple that is to hold God, is led into the temple of the Lord ... Today the Holy of Holies rejoices greatly, and the choir of angels mystically keep feast. With them let us also celebrate the festival today ...*

We do not *remember* the festival, but we *actually* celebrate it in the company of the angelic hosts in heaven. We are never left alone in private interpretation of worship. Together with the angels in heaven, together with the saints, we are ever part of the innumerable Communion.

At this Feast, we again meet an emphasis on the continuity from the Old to the New Testament. They are not on the same level: they cannot be, for the Old cannot overstep the Incarnation of the New. This is a simple truth so often forgotten or misrepresented. The Old Testament may be seen *in actuality* foreshadowing the New. Ever and again, in the Vigil Psalms and readings from the Old Testament, we find the promise of the New, explicitly or figuratively. We love our outspoken, courageous, truthful prophets – as prophets and as men, great in wisdom and staunch in faith. Yet, we never go beyond their own estimation of themselves. To the very days of Christ's own contemporary, St John the Baptist, they all saw themselves in some way as forerunners.

At this Feast, in the three Vespers readings, the prefiguring is particularly striking. In the first reading from Exodus we hear the introduction to the whole theme of the chosen Virgin: she would be the tabernacle holding her child – her God. In image, we perceive the pure womb in the ark of testimony within the tabernacle: ' a cloud covered the tent of the congregation, and the glory of the Lord filled the tabernacle.' The glory of the Lord foreshadows the fullness of the Incarnation to come.

The third reading, from the Prophet Ezekiel, evokes a typically Orthodox interpretation of Old Testament prophecies on the figurative level. Sometimes we see the Old Testament narrative as fact but we interpret it anew, both factually and metaphorically. But, at other times, we are solely concerned with doctrinal interpretation. Here, Ezekiel's vision is primarily important as a preview of the Virgin's giving birth to the Lord in the future:

This gate shall be shut, it will not be opened, and no man shall enter in by it; because the Lord, the God of Israel, hath entered in by it, therefore it shall be shut.

From the allegorical interpretation of Ezekiel's vision, we turn again to the realism of the event, enacted as it were before our eyes:

Today the Mother of God, the Temple that is to hold God, is led into the temple of the Lord.

The word 'Today' presents an immediate demand of our faith and affirms the eternal present. And, because it is so great a Feast and because the Communion of Saints knows no limitation of time:'Today the Holy of Holies rejoices greatly, and the choir of angels mystically keeps feast.'

We are not mere spectators: because there is no barrier of time in worship, we can join in, in fact, we *must* join in: '... let us also celebrate the festival today.' This is no mere commemoration. This is the event. This day sees the introduction to our salvation:

Come, all you people, and let us praise her who alone is undefiled: she who was foretold by the prophets and offered in the temple, the Mother preordained before all ages ...

What makes it even more real and intimate are the constant references to Joachim and Anna. They are the real parents of a real child and they have a right to be proud and rejoice, 'for they have offered unto God, as a three-year-old victim of sacrifice, the Queen without blemish'.

It is indeed a festive scene, a scene of joy and merriment, in which we are invited to participate.

How can we doubt the reality of the event? How deny the invitation?

Rejoice with them, O you mothers: you virgins, dance for joy, and you barren, be of good cheer. For the preordained Queen of all has opened the Kingdom of Heaven to us. Rejoice and be exceeding glad, you peoples.

In like manner, with whatever variations of text, we are consistently reminded throughout the Vigil of the reality of the event. Not only are we reminded, but again and again, we are also invited to participate in the mingling of the immediate and the ageless:

Heaven and earth rejoice, beholding the spiritual Heaven, the only Virgin without blemish, enter the house of God, there to be reared in reverence.

How can we doubt the *reality* of the event in face of such repetitive emphasis on the actuality, the present enactment?

Anna, truly blessed by God's grace, led with gladness into the temple of the Lord the pure and ever-Virgin, who is full of grace, and she called the young girls to go before her, lamps in hand.

There was no lack of oil there to prepare the way for the Most Pure, and at this moment, it is all joy. The agony which is to pierce her heart is hidden within the celebration: 'Her noble parents, Joachim and Anna, leap for joy and dance, for they have borne her that is to bear the Creator.' It is the theological truth which is being celebrated; the factual truth of the dogma. And we are all invited to join in the celebration:

Ye mothers, setting aside every sorrow, follow them in glad-ness, singing the praises of her who became the Mother of God and mediator of joy for the world.

In the Matins of the Feast we are immediately

reminded of the theological basis for our reverent joy: 'Let all of us in faith call her blessed, for she is the Mother of the Lord.' No veneration is allowed for the Mother apart from her Son, either in ikon or text.

Continuity in the divine plan is ever emphasized. The Old predicts the New. The New persists in the history of salvation: 'Let David the Psalmist greatly rejoice.'

In the Matins canons of the Feast, the objectivity of the Feast finds its dramatic expression in the continuous use of the present tense. This Feast day is not merely a day to be remembered lovingly, it is not a day long, long ago, to be remembered dogmatically, but, in the Mystery of the Eternal, it is *now*.

The Feast of 21 November every year occurs as if never before: and every year, afresh, we are invited to participate:

Let us this day hasten together to the Mother of God, honouring her in songs, and let us keep the spiritual feast. For she is offered in the temple as a gift to God.

She is offered *now*, and we are the witnesses *now*.

Glorious sanctuary and holy offering, today the most pure Virgin is dedicated in the temple of God; and in ways which he alone understands, she is kept as a dwelling-place for our God, the King of all.'

The Annunciation (25 March)

Free will is a strongly explicit characteristic of Orthodox spirituality.

From Judas, who chose to betray for no good reason other than his own voluntary decision, to the Mother of God who was given the choice between refusing or accepting the call to be the means of our salvation, we all may choose. The choice is life or death.

Once again, we are confronted by the demand of our texts for our willed participation in the reality of the event. Here is no metaphor, no allegory, no garbled rumour but *fact*. They stand out – the incontrovertible fact of the invitation and the fact of all involved in the personal decision to accept the invitation. It is only too easy to idealize the Annunciation and not face it in its terrifying actuality.

We know from the preceding Feast of the Entry into the Temple that the child Mary had been sedulously guarded from all outside evil. Then, at some time, she would have been removed from the security of the temple and betrothed to Joseph, 'a just man'.

When as his mother Mary was espoused to Joseph, before they came together, she was found with child of the Holy Ghost.

How could this be? Was it by force, was it with her agreement? What happened?

'And in the sixth month the angel Gabriel was sent from God unto a city of Galilee, named Nazareth' (Luke 1:26). This was the sixth month of Elizabeth's conception of St John the Baptist. The Annunciation as told by St Luke is strong, unadorned, factual and certainly in no wise romantic. Gabriel, messenger of God, was sent to 'a virgin espoused to a man whose name was Joseph, of the house of David; and the virgin's name was Mary'. Mary knew nothing of what was coming to her, yet she was immediately 'troubled' at his greeting, wondering what it could mean, what was demanded of her. Then came the divine message – as cryptic, unadorned and demanding as any of the messages received by the prophets of old. She was to conceive and 'bring forth a son, and shalt call his name JESUS.'

It was to be a real birth. Immediately, Mary responds with the one point of human doubt. She accepted the angel without question, and knew that his mission was indeed divine, but there stood out the one questionable, unnatural fact: 'How shall this be seeing I know not a man?'

She was Virgin before birth and Virgin after birth. No human husband was involved. The angel told her 'The Holy Ghost shall come upon thee ...' How else could the Child born of her be Perfect Man and Perfect God? The reality of the seeming paradox is indeed a most vital point in the realism of our Orthodox faith.

The Gospel Truth, the reality of the event, although logically apparently impossible, is emphasized again and again in the text of the Feast. We are faced with the incredible, with no explanation, no ways out into credibility. And we are not only faced with this impossible reality, but we are commanded to bow down and venerate: to venerate the Mother of him whom we worship.

The images of virginity are manifold: the *reality* of the incredible is pounded home in the attributes devised for the Mother of God:

... earth that has not been sown
... burning bush that remains unconsumed
... vessel containing the Nature that cannot be contained
... living City and the spiritual Gate
... living Pavilion of the Glory
... uncut mountain
... throne of the King
... candlestick of the Light
... living Ark of God
... Ladder and Gate
... divine Chariot

Again and again the images for our veneration simultaneously point precisely to our theological stand regarding the Mother of God: our veneration is never too far removed from our objective doctrine. For the Mother of God we have no veneration as a person *in her own right*. She is always overtly connected (emphatically so) with her voluntary self-sacrifice, her courage and her purity, which allowed her to be the Mother of our God. Only *vis à vis* his Incarnation is her importance stressed.

'Behold the handmaid of the Lord.' We take her self-sacrifice literally. We reverence her for her faithful obedience to the Divine Word. The Mother of God is no myth for us. She is *real* – real in her fear, her amazement, and in her obedience. Brought up in the temple, dedicated by her parents, she is ready to face an irate bridegroom, ignominy, shame, perhaps even death – all the terrors of childbirth without marriage. All this she faces, not metaphorically or allegorically, but in reality.

In the first place she even has to face the terror of the angelic apparition: 'Why does your figure blaze with fire?' Naturally, as a real young girl, she would be frightened by the appearance of the angel.

During Vespers, we hear again the variety of paradoxical names addressed to the Virgin:

... unsearchable depth
... bridge that leads to heaven
... ladder raised on high
... divine jar of manna

And from image into function:

... deliverance from the curse
... restoration of Adam

At her meeting with Gabriel, Mary is as bewildered as any young girl would be. She is no figment of religious devotion or, even worse, sentimentality. She is *real* and her fright and puzzlement are real.

> *How, tell me, shall I become the spacious habitation and the holy place of him that rides upon the cherubim? Do not beguile me with deceit: for I have not known pleasure, I have not entered into wedlock. How then shall I bear a child?*

The Feast of the Annunciation certainly conveys the immediate sense of bewilderment, fear, and faith that contains doubt. Even the messenger, Gabriel, is no cardboard figure: he too, sent as he was to give 'the glad tidings of her conceiving', could not really grasp the practicality of his message. 'How shall he who dwells in the heights, whom none can comprehend, be born of a virgin? How shall he whose throne is heaven and whose footstool is the earth be held in the womb of a woman?' Yet, he is true to the trust put in him – *consciously.*

How, on this occasion, the Gospel text is hammered into us! There is no room for questioning of the event's having really taken place. At Vespers, at Great Compline, at Matins, in simple repetition, hardly varied, the truth, in all its unwatered-down reality, is taught to the faithful Christian.

In the sixth month, the chief of the angelic hosts was sent to you, pure Virgin ...

In the sixth month, Gabriel, the Archangel, was sent from heaven to the city of Nazareth ...

The angel Gabriel was sent from heaven by God to the city of Nazareth ...

All is sung relentlessly, in the same tone: the true faith, over and over again.

Nor are we allowed to minimize the reality of the Virgin's faith, her blind obedience and courage in the face of the awesome message given to her. We cannot fall into any idealistic cult, or see her as image or metaphor of any kind: she is a pure, real maiden. She is terrified, but her terror is contained within unflinching faith.

We find it difficult enough at times to hold to our faith even with the whole life of Christ to uphold us. She had faith *before* the event: 'accepting the salutation with faith, she conceived you the pre eternal God'. There is no grudging admission or evading of the issue by symbolic explanations: in her we have the pattern of *lived* faith, real faith, suffering and courageous faith. At this Feast of the Mother of

27

God, we acknowledge wholeheartedly our debt to her. 'From you, Christ our God and our salvation has taken human nature, raising it up into himself.'

Is it surprising that, as a result, we turn to her for her intercession? 'Pray to him that our souls may be saved.' Intercession is a mystery. Of course we pray to Christ directly. Yet we also know that we are told to pray for each other. Who better then than his own Mother, without whose obedience to the divine invitation we should never have seen him?

Throughout the Canon of Matins, the theme of the Virgin's natural bewilderment and fear is retained: her meeting with the archangel has an immediate effect of real presence. Mary questions. Gabriel answers. For example:

THE MOTHER OF GOD: O Angel, help me to understand the meaning of your words. How shall what you say come to pass? Tell me clearly, how shall I conceive, who am a virgin maid? And how shall I become the Mother of my Maker?

GABRIEL: You think, so it seems, that I utter words deceitfully; and I rejoice to see your prudence. But take courage, O Lady: for when God wills, strange wonders are easily accomplished.

In such dramatic form, the immediacy of the event becomes even more pronounced: the meeting of maid and angel is now real – compelling our attention and our participation in the event.

When the young maiden questions, as it were, the actual practicality of Gabriel's message, even as thousands of people subsequently have questioned the manner of her giving birth, the answer she gets is unrelenting in its simple demand not for common sense but for faith: 'O Virgin, you seek to know from me the manner of your conceiving, but this is beyond all interpretation ...' Reasoning cannot help. We must be willing to accept the truth without worrying about the details which will surely offend common sense. The young maiden is destined 'alone among women' to preserve the seal of her virginity, 'while yet receiving in your womb the pre-eternal Word and Lord'.

The dialogue continues between maid and angel: she is so natural in her repeated questioning of the situation: 'Tell me truly: how shall I, my purity remaining untouched, bear in my flesh the Word that has no body?' And, at each query, the Archangel in effect gives the identical response: '... in his good pleasure, the Word of God shall descend upon you, as dew upon the fleece'.

After the questioning comes the radiance of pure martyrdom: again, this is no cardboard saint, but the real Mother of God who sees through all the horror of her practical situation to the radiance beyond: 'I am filled with divine joy. For you speak to me of joy, a joy without end.' Joy? Her son on the Cross, treachery, unbelief, her whole sacrifice in years to come to be scrutinized and discarded as unscientific fable? We might well think it a strange joy for one who is acclaimed by the archangel as the one through whom God's promise to Abraham 'receives its fulfilment'.

One of the most beautiful of our hymns is sung as the *Kontakion* in Matins of this Feast of the Annunciation. It is sung at other times, but here is its rightful place, the acknowledgment of the Mother of God's place in the history of our human salvation:

Mighty conquering warrior Mother of God, we your servants whom you have freed from ills, offer up to you songs of thanksgiving, and with your unconquerable power deliver us from all afflictions, that we may cry to you, Hail Bride unwedded.

Bride unwedded: the root and stem of our Faith. Christ: Perfect God and Perfect Man.

Although this Feast falls in the Great Lent, fish, wine and oil are permitted on this day. The Feast takes over from the Fast. How could it not in the presence of the Promise of the Son of God taking his human body from the Virgin?

The Feast of the Assumption (15 August)

Strictly speaking, 'The Assumption' is not the Orthodox name for this beloved and solemn Feast.

When our monastery was founded, we were somewhat daunted at the thought of the literal translation of its name from the Greek or the Slavonic – 'The Monastery of the Falling Asleep of the Mother of God' would certainly have seemed strange to English ears, not to mention the feelings of a rural postman! Hence we adopted the more common Western term of 'the Assumption'. But the nuance of meaning between *Assumption* and *Falling Asleep* speaks volumes for the immediate undoctrinal realism of our attitude of faith.

We know that she died – that she fell asleep. But we cannot know, as we know of Christ's Ascension, that she, at death, was received into heaven, as a person. There is no Gospel evidence, only Apocryphal.

The fact that we do not accept the doctrine of the Assumption *as* doctrine certainly does not hinder us from venerating the Mother of God in her life on earth – and continuing such veneration into her life in heaven: 'What is this present feast? "Christ ... has translated into the heavenly mansions her who bore him without seed ..." ' Or again: 'The honoured choir of the wise apostles was miraculously assembled to bury in glory your most pure body ...'. Miraculously, because according to the Apocryphal version, the apostles, dead and alive, assembled from all the ends of the earth to witness the falling asleep of the Mother of God, and her ascent into heaven.

In veneration, we wholly acknowledge and gladly confess what we will not allow in official dogmatic teaching. A strange dichotomy perhaps, for critical eyes even not critically honest, but one that emphasizes the reality of the *experience* in worship. Although not necessarily directly connected with canonical precision, this expression is an act of love, of living faith, of centuries of tradition outside the Canons of the Church, or, at any rate, constituting a popular supplement.

The sentiments sung and prayed at this Feast are above all a real expression of theologically unfounded popular devotion, not met with elsewhere in this precise form. The real Mother must be given a very special death – not like that of any other mortal.

> *The glorious apostles knew you, O Virgin without spot, to be a mortal woman and at the same time, beyond and above nature, the Mother of God: therefore they touched you with fearful hands, as they gazed upon you shining with glory, the tabernacle that had held God.*

The tabernacle that had held God – this phrase is so typical of the repetitive Orthodox attitude of religious objectivity. We may extol the Mother of God with every epithet of beauty in our vocabulary but the *real* reason for such praise lies not in her *as* her, but as the one who voluntarily chose the martyrdom of bearing God. Not only did she choose, but she was chosen – and this is a yet more important point reiterated throughout our veneration. How can we not venerate in reality her who in reality was chosen of all women to be the Mother of our incarnate God? 'For Christ our God who cannot be contained was pleased to be contained in you.' It is an exciting, exhilarating exchange. She, the Mother of God, is indeed blessed and is so pure that she enters into the purity of heaven with body incorrupt. But we too are blessed, for once again reunited with her Son, can she not pray for us, sinners as we are? Can she not bring our pleas to him?

We treat the question of intercession very simply. We pray for each other, for our parents, children and friends. We have been told to pray. What difference can

31

mortal death make to the current of prayer? We continue to pray for the dead, and we expect those in heaven to pray for us. If a mother can pray for her children on earth, how much more can the Mother of Christ our God pray to him on our behalf?

Blessed also are we in having you as our succour: for day and night you intercede for us, and the sceptres of kings are strengthened by your supplications.

The Mother of God is our greatest comfort. Where our prayer can only ever be inadequate, for we remain fallen human creatures, she fills in the inevitable gaps.

We find it strange that for some Christians, the Mother of God is a stumbling block in the way of their worship of Christ God. She is not a rival goddess! Even as we might well ask a friend to pray for us, as indeed we all pray for each other (or should do), so we ask her, again and again, to pray for us. All prayers, we have been told, are acceptable, but if in heavenly terms there is any equivalent to human values, then what could be more valuable than the prayers of his own Mother?

In our veneration of her, we call to mind all our previous images:

... bright candlestick, flaming with immaterial fire
... golden censer burning with divine gold
... vessel of manna
... rod of Aaron
... holy ark and table of the bread of life

We venerate her in all reality, but always and only in her relationship to her Divine Son. This cannot be over-stressed.

At this Feast we remember that death for the faithful may be awesome, may be and mostly is full of the grief of parting, but the grief is ever temporary. Death has no dominion over us and the joy of life eternal, where she is already, awaits us:

He has made her dwell in the heavenly abodes. Dancing with her in her joy, we cry aloud unto Christ: 'Blessed are You, O most glorious God, our God and the God of our fathers' ... the Tabernacle of the glory of God is translated in Zion to a heavenly abode, where the pure voices of those that keep feast are heard with a sound of ineffable joy ...

As the stylized drama unfolds, the inner excitement grows, the warmth of the Feast permeates our very being. We are all invited to join in this inexpressible festivity:

O young men and virgins, old men and rulers, kings and judges, who honour the memory of the Virgin and Mother of God, sing: Blessed are you, O Lord God of our fathers.

We are all invited to this holy gaiety and so too is the whole of nature:

Let the high mountains ring out to the trumpet of the Spirit: let the hills now rejoice and let the apostles of God dance for joy. The Queen goes to dwell with her Son and to rule with him for ever.

What ineffable triumph of majesty! The Queen ... the Royal Son ... and the Kingdom which will not perish. Yet the realism of the duality of death and life must never be forgotten even in the excitement of the experience of life in death. Christ's was a *real* death and his was a *real* tomb. Likewise, the Mother of God's death was no fiction, no mirage, but *real*. Thus, even as we rejoice in her life in heaven, we acknowledge her death on earth:

Come, O ye faithful, let us approach the tomb of the Mother of God, and let us embrace it, touching it sincerely with the lips and eyes and foreheads of the heart.

If we believe in the reality of death and in the reality of a living heaven – if we accept all the Christian paradox, then miracles are not fantasies but objective

33

manifestations of the everlasting presence of Christ. No miracle can be severed from Christ's miracles: the miracles of today are a reflection, an echo, a repetition of his, not of human origin but of the Holy Spirit. They happen *outside* our volition rather than by any human will or intention.

The Holy Spirit works with the generosity of the Sower in the parable (Mark 4:1–20), sowing his seed in unlikely places where there is no palpable return or reward or even gratitude. Hence we, the Orthodox, are a little chary of accepting any idiorhythmic contemporary claims of personal healing gifts. Miracles there are from 'accredited' sources – particularly from the grace bestowed by ikons of the Mother of God – but the miracle-working that has come down to us over the ages, has been seasoned, as it were, even by blood of martyrs.

Miracles worked by saints did come sometimes in their life-time but more assuredly after their death. The miracle-working ikons and the miracle-working saints are all *within* the Church. We are disinclined in the first instance to accept anything or anyone in the field of miracles *outside* the Church and its whole vast but simple framework. In effect, we avoid the individualism whose claims are unrelated fundamentally to the objective main body of worship. In the Feast of the Assumption, as in all things, we declare the reality of the miraculous:

O you apostles, assembled here from the ends of the earth, bury my body in Gethsemane: and You, O my Son and God, receive my spirit.

A real death, a real burial – these are followed by the final reality: the taking up into heaven of the blessed body without awaiting the Last Judgment:

At a divine command the chief apostles hastened from the ends of the earth to bury you ...

Somehow, in our veneration of the Mother of God, we

34

pack in all our faith and our overflowing love for her Son, and our trust in a heavenly world which will fulfil all that is good in this. In the acknowledgment of the Mother of God's unique life and death, there is a simple faith going far beyond all the intricacies of so-called theological disputation:

By your holy Falling Asleep, O Virgin Mother and Bride of God, you, who gave birth to the Life, have been transported into immortal life, attended by angels, principalities, and powers, by apostles, prophets, and the whole creation: and your Son received into his immaculate hands your spotless soul.

Passages such as this show the unanimity of ikon and holy text. Both are theological in the truest sense, one expressed in word, the other in form – to the ear and to the eye. But, both are to be interpreted in precisely the same manner irrespective of form; both demand the appreciation of the reality of the event.

Hence, in the falling asleep of the Mother of God it is not inappropriate that the *Prokimenon* before the Gospel should recall the earlier Feast of the Annunciation: 'My soul doth magnify the Lord, and my spirit hath rejoiced in God my Saviour.'

What is the essence of the Orthodox attitude to the Mother of God?

Christ was asked where he lived. What was his answer? 'Come and see.' This answer still obtains. What can be more objectively real than the very act of worship which no words can adequately describe?

How do we approach the Mother of God?

Shut your books. Go to any Orthodox Church on a Feast day of the Mother of God. 'Come and see.' You will probably find a crowd of Cypriot faithful, mostly women and old men, the women in black with black scarves on their heads; here and there a younger one in brighter clothing; a small child looking round in wonder from bright, dark brown eyes; a blaze of candles held in the hands of the faithful; incense. And the song goes up from hearts uplifted in devotion – the

ancient rite of devotion to the Mother of God – the
Paraclesis is being celebrated:

Most Holy Mother of God
Save us.

Chapter 3

Feasts of Our Lord I

BEFORE THE ENTRY INTO JERUSALEM

The Nativity of our Lord Jesus Christ
(25 December)

Christ is born!

There is an immediate surge of joy, excitement, reverence, praise and gratitude: only to be repeated later after the darkness of death.

Now there is a baby, a real baby and a real mother. But it is a real baby within the Mystery of real baby and real God. Born of a woman certainly but with no human father. The Holy Spirit came upon Mary and she conceived in her womb. We are faced with a divine miracle.

In our Christmas services, in our hymns and prayers of the day, we give full measure to this Mystery of real birth, but with no human father. This is expressed in the reactions of Joseph, the bridegroom, to the shock of his young maiden bride's pregnancy.

Before they came together, Mary was with child. Justifiably, Joseph was extremely angry and bewildered: he had taken this pure young girl to be his wife and what was the outcome? The imminent birth of a child before their marriage was consummated.

On the Eve of the Feast, during the Royal Hours, we hear Joseph's bewilderment and anger. Our services contain a realistic picture of his wretchedness verging on the satirical: he was a just man and did not want to hurt his young bride and yet the situation was unbearable! In the First Hour, Joseph is most outspoken in his reproaches:

What kind of event, Mary, is happening in you? I am amazed and astounded, and sorely grieved in mind! ... I received you as blameless before the Lord from the Priests of the temple: and what do I see?

Yet, even as Joseph laments, the *Kontakion* (the hymn of the day) is repeatedly sung, in the melody of the imperial Tone III:

Today the Virgin comes to the cave, to give birth to the Word eternal, in manner inexpressible. Rejoice, O world, to hear this, glorify with the angels and the shepherds, the longed-for coming, the new-born Child, God before the ages.

In the Third Hour, Joseph is questioned: 'Tell us, Joseph, how did you take the Virgin from the Holy of Holies and bring her with child to Bethlehem?' He remains sorely puzzled but the anger seems to have left him, and he is prepared to accept the situation, to believe 'that in ways inexplicable Mary would give birth to God'.

However, in the Sixth Hour, doubt and astonishment seize Joseph again. Mary, a Virgin, comes to Bethlehem to 'give birth to the Lord' – choirs of angels precede her. Joseph, seeing all this, is struck with horror and amazement:

O Virgin, what is this strange mystery in you? And how will you give birth, Heifer unblemished, untried by the yoke?

So far, Mary has not reacted to the chiding of the bridegroom, but when we come to the Ninth Hour the rôles are reversed, and it is now Mary who takes her turn to rebuke. She chides Joseph with his unbelief and proclaims her own faith in what is being born of her.

The Magnificat, at the Feast of the Annunciation, was her statement of blind obedience. But now, with the child stirring within her, comes the reality of love and faith: in *her* baby, *her* God. It is a most beautiful hymn of triumph sung in Tone II, the Tone reserved for grief and surely significant therefore of the glorious divine paradox to come: womb – tomb, birth – crucifixion, life – Life.

So far we have encountered the reality of the *heralding* of the birth. Now follows the confession of the actuality of the birth as depicted in the Vigil of the Feast. The Vigil normally comprises Great Compline and Matins although this does not always obtain but is ruled by the day of the week on which the Feast falls. The Vigil service demands the acknowledgment of the actual event on the actual day: 'Today for man's sake is seen in the flesh he who by nature is invisible.' The *reality* of the baby is emphasized and re-emphasized even as a prelude to the coming reality of crucifixion and resurrection. If at this inaugural stage there were any doubt of his being a real human baby, then crucifixion and resurrection would lose their literal meaning and we would indeed be building our house on the sand of mythology: '... Jesus bowed the heavens and came down, and without changing he took up his dwelling in a Virgin womb ...'

Now the wise men from the East play their part, coming to worship the baby with their gifts, acknowledging his divinity: shepherds behold the wonder and the wise men offer their ominous gifts:

... and eagerly opening their treasures, they offered to him precious gifts: refined gold, as to the King of the ages, and frankincense, as to the God of all; and myrrh they offered to the Immortal, as to one three days dead.

The reality of the theological connection between birth and crucifixion persists: gifts to the baby just born are the identical gifts of the precious spices for the man just crucified. Baby and Man: God Immortal.

The history of our salvation is being in reality enacted at the moment of this birth. '... the ancient condemnation of Adam is loosed. Paradise is opened to us: the serpent is laid low.' Paradise in actuality will not be opened until the thief will accompany the living Christ, but already, at the moment of his birth, that moment of the promise of eternal life is present: 'Paradise is opened to us: the serpent is laid low.'

The new Eve, Mary, Mother of God, is the human passage, the human highway, for our human salvation. The serpent recognizes this threatening development:

Of old he deceived the woman in Paradise, but now he sees a woman become Mother of the Creator.

The boundless jigsaw puzzle of human destiny has all its pieces for the history of our salvation. And, in the centre of the puzzle, lies the most important piece – the baby in a manger:

He looses the bands of sin, and through becoming child he heals Eve's pangs in travail. Therefore let all creation sing and dance for joy, for Christ has come to restore it and to save our souls.

The swaddling clothes are wrapped round tightly. The bands of sin are thereby loosened.

It cannot be over-emphasized how for the Orthodox the Feast persists over the centuries as an immediate *living* event, repeated year after year after year with the same freshness of divine novelty: everything is in the *present*; is happening *now*; is *real*.

Doctrine does not exist apart from event. And we are all invited to participate in this glorious celebration:

Come, O ye faithful, and let us behold where Christ is born. Let us join the Wise Men from the East, and follow the guiding star.

It is happening *now* – not in history. And it is *now* that his mother Mary remains steadfastly faithful to her initial obedience. Of course – for she is a real woman – even at this last minute before giving birth, she is puzzled, and depends entirely on her unflinching faith for strength:

'I have not known man: how then shall I bear a child? Who has ever seen a birth without seed?' But, as it is written, 'Where God so wills, the order of nature is overcome'. Christ is born of the Virgin in Bethlehem of Judah.

Is born, *now*. True history – and true present.

The Matins Canon emphasizes and re-emphasizes the one theme of God's condescension. Christ: true God, true Man. His unbelievable love for mankind – betrayed at the Fall, betrayed again at the crucifixion. He comes to save us:

Man fell from the divine and better life: though made in the image of God, through transgression he became wholly subject to corruption and decay. But now the wise Creator fashions him anew ...

It is on all counts the redeeming of the human race:

God is mingled with the form of mortal man, and so he looses the unhappy womb of Eve from the bitter curse of old.

So too, in taking upon himself true humanity, Christ has in mysterious fashion made us partakers in the divine nature. This is indeed a Mystery and we must not probe it too far, nor give it rigid outlines. Digging with feet of clay is a dangerous pastime. We might well fall into the pit of heresy.

Yet the Mystery *is* there; not to be defined, but never forgotten. We are raised above the beasts of the world. We are not beasts, nor are beasts human. Nor is nature. All the various heresies and near heresies – tree and flower veneration, flirtations with non-Christian cults and religions – all are rooted in ignoring or forgetting the Incarnation and the duty, as well as the blessing, thereby imposed upon us as Christians. God became true Man – without sin. We sin, but our humanity is blessed:

O Christ, who have made yourself in the form of a creature of vile clay, by your sharing in that which is worse, even our flesh, you have made us partakers in the divine nature; for you have become mortal man, yet still remain God.

41

And, there comes the repeated, immediate excitement, the enthusiasm engendered by the actuality of the event. Not for a moment do we cease to be present at the Feast: it is happening as for the very first time and each one of us, however humble, however unworthy, is a privileged witness.

Imagery mingles with common language in the texts of the Feast: imagery, not only to demonstrate and emphasize the glory of the event, but also to bring it into historical relationship. Again and again the words of the Christmas texts recall the Old Testament, seeing the events of the Old as the foreshadowing of the New, and the New as the justification of the Old.

What the prophets suffered, what the kings and rulers experienced, now make their fullest sense in what is happening at this very instant as the baby is born from an unwedded Virgin:

From the Mountain overshadowed by the forest you have come, made flesh from her that knew not wedlock.

O Christ, whom Jacob foretold in days of old, calling you the Expectation of the nations ...

As dew upon the fleece you have descended into the womb of the Virgin ...

O Virgin, sprung from the root of Jesse ...

In the midst of allegory, poetry and imagery there is ever a strong realism. Here, even as the laudatory poetry pours forth, there comes the reminder of the actual event: Virgin she was, and Virgin remains, but the *place* of birth was ordained in obedience 'to the decree of Caesar'. As man, the baby Christ was enrolled amongst the servants of Caesar. All went to be enrolled – and God himself was taken to be enrolled. What could be more convincing than this? He is true God – *and* True Man. But his Mother remains a Virgin.

Repeatedly the Christmas service brings us back

sharply to this point of Christ being true God and true Man. It takes us to the moment of his birth, to the moment of renewed hope of Paradise: '… let us hasten to this place where now is born a young Child, the pre-eternal God'. The Feast is not only a celebration but it is a driving force: Christ *is* born, not *was*. We must do something about it *now*. Christ *is* born. There is no past tense in the miracle of the Feast.

But it is not only a matter of hastening gladly to the Feast, of being present in body in order to worship and glorify Christ, our God. Christ is born as a human baby and we are there to greet him in his Incarnation, to love him actively as One present with us, to show our deepest gratitude to him for being born of his own will in a state of true embodiment that he might be our salvation. Even as we bow down before him, we are there also to thank his Mother for agreeing to the terrible thing demanded of her:

Today the Master is born as a babe of a Virgin Mother.

Today the Virgin bears the Master within the cave.

Today shepherds behold the Saviour …

Today the Master … is wrapped as a babe in swaddling rags.

Today all creation rejoices …

Today is the significant word. This is no memory, no allegory, no religious fable, no event in the past. Yes, it is an *event* in the past but equally it is happening now. Eternity is condescending into time:

Today Christ is born of the Virgin in Bethlehem. Today he who knows no beginning now begins to be, and the Word is made flesh. The powers of heaven greatly rejoice, and the earth with mankind makes glad. The Magi offer gifts, the shepherds proclaim the marvel, and we cry aloud without ceasing: Glory to God in the highest, and on earth peace, good will among men.

43

The Meeting of our Lord and God and Saviour Jesus Christ (2 February)

Why 'Meeting'? It does seem a strange word to use in English but in fact Meeting is a direct translation of the Greek and Slavonic names for this Feast. As ever, it is a practical rather than dogmatic term.

What Meeting? Christ God, as an infant, is carried by his Mother into the temple to be presented to his people. He is received into the arms of the Elder, Simeon:

Simeon received in his embrace the Word uncircumscribed and supreme in being, who is borne on high in glory upon a heavenly throne.

From the moment that the Vigil of the Feast begins, we are drawn into the double theological truth of real baby and real God. As a real baby, according to the Law, his Mother presents him in the temple, and at that very instant, he is recognized by Simeon as the long-awaited moment of the completion of his years of serving and waiting in the temple:

Lord, now lettest thou thy servant depart in peace according to thy word: for mine eyes have seen thy salvation ...

What a moment of joy! What a moment of dread! Simeon hardly dared to touch the Infant – so real and so divine. The Mother of the Child also knows who he is, but also does her duty as a faithful Jewish mother as she places her baby in the arms of the Elder. Hence, God is *meeting* his people. He is meeting Simeon who represents the people with whom he has chosen to dwell in his Incarnation, who will be the first to receive him – and the first to crucify him.

What we celebrate is the *meeting* of the divine and the human so that the history of salvation may take its next step from the initial step of the divine birth.

The birth in the stable was a Mystery hidden from the world at large – witnessed by animals, a few shepherds and the wise men from the East. In some ways the manger was as secret as the tomb would be later. But, even as the public affair of the trial and crucifixion preceded the privacy of the resurrection, so now the birth in the cave is openly acknowledged at the Meeting – as later we should cry aloud 'Christ is Risen'.

The human journey of Christ God has taken its first overt step at this Meeting with his people in his temple. The text of the Feast consistently emphasizes this inaugural significance:

> *He who is without beginning, the Word of the Father, has made a beginning in time without forsaking his divinity, and as a baby forty days old he is of his own will brought by the Virgin his Mother as an offering in the temple of the Lord.*

This is only one passage of many of the same import – and what a wealth of theology is packed into these simple words! The *essence* of the Creed is here and the *continuity* from Old to New. Above all, we find in this Feast of the Meeting the eternal paradox of the Father and the Son: two Persons, but One God. Thus Christ, 'As Maker of the Law he fulfils the Law'.

We cannot avoid the paradox; we cannot hide behind theological niceties; we are forced into facing our faith: either we believe in the incomprehensible, or we do not. Either, in total humility, we accept what is beyond our comprehension, or we do not. There is no middle way: 'Today he who once gave the Law to Moses on Sinai submits himself to the ordinances of the Law.' It is no accident that later on Moses will be seen present at the Transfiguration.

The texts of the Feast allow for no possibility of being softened or made palatable to human reasoning. We cannot accept their consistent dialectic unless we become as little children and accept logical contradictions without submitting them to a process of immanent scrutiny. The baby in Simeon's arms, in effect, is making manifest to us that our adult reasoning must be laid aside once and for all if we are to meet him as our Saviour.

What an impossible demand on one level! Why impossible? Possibly because the demand is so simple – it allows for no side roads on which we might slip away and yet assure ourselves that we are keeping to the main road. Simeon knew who the baby was; he did not doubt but 'with exceeding joy received him in his outstretched arms'. Yet, this receiving of his God was synonymous for Simeon with his own death. There was no point in his going on with life after such a moment, a moment that could not be repeated, a moment for which he had waited year after year. Hence his repeated prayer, 'Lord, now lettest thou thy servant depart in peace according to thy word.'

We are not all ready to depart, but for Simeon it is as if years of bondage fall away – years of waiting, of longing, of preparation for this precious moment, of prayer, of fasting, and, perhaps, times of grey despondency when it must have seemed all an illusion that would never be fulfilled: 'Now am I set free, for I have beheld my Saviour.'

The text of the Feast persists in pointing out to us the importance of the Mother of God in her relationship to her Son. We love her already for her unbelievable courage in accepting the message of the archangel that she would be the Virgin Mother of a child. We love her for her courage in the face of Joseph's reproaches and now we see her in the same unwavering attitude of faith – unquestioning of the Lord's command and doing her duty in all humility.

The holy temple of God holds the holy things of God, but the Mother of God, in quiet obedience, is a living Temple: she has actually held God in her womb. And now, what greater proof of her obedience, of her loving humility, than this Feast? She takes none of his glory to herself:

Today the holy Mother who is higher than any temple, has come into the temple, disclosing to the world the Maker of the world and Giver of the Law.

It is his Feast, but so too his Mother's glory. And it is all *real*; not an image: '... not in fancy nor in imagination but in very truth he has appeared to the world.' He has appeared, but he would not have done so if not for her obedience. An interesting side-light: God does not work against our will. We could not be saved if the young Virgin had refused, as she might well have done out of fear, out of doubt, if for no other reason than all the practical dangers involved. Again and again, we come up against the self-effacing figure of the Mother of God: 'The Mother who has never known wedlock has brought into the temple him who shone forth before the ages from the Father ...' She *knew* nothing: she simply believed.

The juxtaposition of God and Man is unbelievably exciting and ever anew. What can be more true, more obvious and yet more astonishing than the outspoken paradox:

The Ancient of Days, a young child in the flesh, was brought to the temple by his Mother the Virgin, fulfilling the ordinance of his own Law.

Christ condescended as Man, to fulfil his own Law as God. That thought alone could be food for meditation for the rest of our lives. But, even as the sower scattered his seed, God is prodigal, even in the food he gives us for thought.

The Vigil Service of the Feast is not only concerned with the inner paradoxical theology, it is also the mouthpiece of sheer veneration, of worship, of praise. Whole passages call us to re-live in glad excitement this divine event. It is a Feast. Let us rejoice:

Adorn your bridal chamber, O Zion, and welcome Christ the King: salute Mary, the heavenly gate. For she has been made as the throne of the cherubim, and she carries the King of glory. A cloud of light is the Virgin, who has borne in the flesh the Son begotten before the morning star ...

Prayer and poetry merge in devotion. But strangely enough, for all our exuberant praise of the Mother of God, we keep strictly within theological bounds, even at a Feast such as this when we extol and praise her continuously. The bounds are her total humanity – and we only worship God in Three Persons. The distinction is ever and again made clear: we never make the Mother of God anything but fully human. Thereby in one way we love her the more, because she is no mythical goddess or semi-divine, but one of us. Yet she dared what none of us would dare, and, moreover, mortal as she was, she alone was chosen of God to be his Mother:

We magnify you, Christ the giver of life, and we venerate your most pure Mother ...

We *venerate* – respect, admire, give her due attention, set her apart from the rest of us, but never, in any sense, grant her any supernatural attribute or quasi-goddess rank! No worship of a human creature is permissible.

Another aspect of this Feast is the divine condescension which acknowledges and pities human doubts and fears. We are ever inclined to explain away what we cannot fully comprehend. To avoid the heresy of seeing Christ as God with only the *appearance* of humanity (thus, if nothing else, denying the truth of the crucifixion) this Feast emphasizes Christ's reality as a baby. In fact, this Feast is most important as a balance, a refutation of exaggerated anti-Arianism which ends up in docetism and two extremes of heresy: semblance of God and semblance of man. The Feast affirms the one Truth: Christ is true God and true Man. Hence:

God the most pure receives purification, that he may confirm the reality of the human flesh which he took from the Virgin.

The humanity from his Mother is *true* humanity. The Divinity from his Father is *true* divinity. Simeon knew this: 'Let me depart: for I have seen you, the Life of all.' There was nothing more for Simeon to experience in this life which seemed to him to be of any value. What could there be when he had once held God in his arms?

... for mine eyes have seen thy salvation, which thou hast prepared before the face of all people; a light to lighten the Gentiles, and the glory of thy people Israel.

Old and New combined in Simeon's arms: the New, the fulfilment of the Old, the justification of all the prophets who had gone before Simeon and died in expectation of what now had come to pass.

Sometimes, our texts take on a realism which is quite unexpected. It is true that Simeon is believed to have been an old man at the time of this Feast, but the verisimilitude of some of the attributes devised for him might strike the onlooker as a little strange! Delightfully realistic pictures such as: '... and you, the feeble legs of the Elder, run straight to meet Christ.' There is, in fact, constant reference made to Simeon's old age and this lends an even more tender touch to his evident devotion to the Mother of God: he 'bent down and reverently touched the foot-prints of the Mother of God who knew not wedlock ...' – a picture of pure humility on the part of the old priest.

This Feast is not all joy. The Cross is there. The prophecy of dread comes to the infant's Mother – the purpose of his divine birth:

And a sword shall pierce your heart, O All-Pure Virgin.

Was it not enough that she had to bear a child in a stable? That her betrothed husband doubted her innocence? That she was to see the Son grow and behave in a manner unaccountable – already as a child disputing in the temple? She was yet to see that Child crucified, a felon on either side. We cannot love and respect her too much:

Fulfilling the written Law, he who loves mankind is now brought into the temple.

Year after year, we sing our gratitude and praise to the Virgin, Mother of God, and always afresh as if for the very first time:

That which is fulfilled in you is beyond the understanding of angels and mortal man, O pure Virgin Mother. In the shadow and letter of the Law we discern a sign; every first-born male that opens the womb is holy to God. Therefore we magnify the first-born Son and Word of the unbegun Father, become the first-born of a Mother who knew no man.

The Holy Theophany
(6 January)

Being today in the streams of the Jordan, the Lord cried out to John: do not fear to baptize me, for I have come to save Adam the first-formed.

As at every Feast, we find ourselves at the centre of a real action. Today it is God's manifestation (Theophany) of himself to his people. For the Orthodox, the Feast of the Theophany has a different emphasis from the Western Feast of the Epiphany celebrated on the same day. For us, the importance of the Feast does not lie in God's manifestation of himself to the Gentiles (our wise men came already, at Christmas). But in his manifestation of himself – God in Three Persons. The importance of course also lies in the institution of Christian baptism by his own example. If God himself chose to be baptized, how dare we deny baptism to ourselves or to our children?

It is a never-ending source of surprise for Orthodox parents that other parents can actually postpone their children's baptism for months or even years, or even deny their responsibility, asserting that the child, when it grows up, should 'choose for himself'. This same parent no doubt ensures that the child is vaccinated and inoculated at every *physically* vulnerable point. So often, spiritual danger has not the same stark reality as physical. Of course, it does not have the visible and displeasing signs such as a scarlet fever rash or smallpox eruptions. However, we approach our faith in a way which may even horrify a non-Orthodox spectator.

At baptism, the baby is actually submitted to liberation from any possible demonic presence: 'Expel from him (her) every evil and unclean spirit which hides and makes its lair in his (her) heart.' Moreover, the one to be baptized, or the god-parent for an infant, is asked the direct question: 'Do you renounce Satan, and all his works, and all his angels, and all his service and all his pride?' The answer, 'I do renounce him!'

This salvation through baptism, this setting free from the Devil and all his works, and the subsequent responsibility as a Christian, is not a humanly devised formula; it would have little meaning without the Gospel precedent celebrated at the Feast of the Theophany: the *actual* Baptism of God Incarnate himself.

The Feast of the Theophany asserts the reality of the Baptism of God – and with it the explicit reality of the theology of the Trinity. It is no abstract creed, no theoretical dogma, nothing devised by the human intelligence but a simple actuality:

In the Jordan, your baptism, O Lord, disclosed the worship of the Trinity. For the voice of the Father witnessed to you, naming you the beloved Son: and the Spirit, in the likeness of a dove, assured the firmness of the word. O Christ God, having shown yourself, and given light to the world, glory to you.

In pattern, the Theophany Feast follows that of Christmas. Once again we have the preparation on the Eve in the Royal Hours, and the repetitive use of the present tense emphasizes the reality:

Today the nature of the waters is made holy: and the Jordan breaks asunder, and draws back the streams of its own waters, for it sees the Master who makes himself clean.

As ever this is the reiteration of our faith: Christ is God and Christ is Man and he makes himself clean.

But, if Christ descends into the water to be baptized because he *is* Christ, the consequence is inevitable – he surely is baptized but, by his presence in the water, the water is made holy. He institutes the blessing of water to make it holy – holy water for further baptism, for bodily and spiritual health, and for the blessing of homes, animals and ships.

The concept of holy water emanating from the one occasion of God standing in the midst of the Jordan to be baptized is a revelation of God the Trinity:

Today the Trinity, our God, reveals himself to us indivisible: for the Father distinctly proclaimed confirmation of the relationship: the Spirit, in likeness a dove, came down from heaven: the Son bent down his pure head to the Forerunner: and, in baptism, delivered man from slavery, for he loves mankind.

The Service of the Royal Hours is immediate and dramatic, making us thrill to the real presence of God demanding baptism from his creature. It is so vivid, so real, that we can hardly conceive a life in which baptism plays no part. We might be there on the banks of the River Jordan as we hear sung in that tone which joins earth to heaven, Tone VIII:

Thus speaks the Lord to John: Prophet, come and baptize me, who created you: who enlightened with grace and cleansed all: touch my divine head, and do not hesitate ...

The River Jordan itself comes to life in this awesome experience: its streams turn back and in dread cannot flow forward in their natural course:

I am not used to wash him who is clean, I have not learned how to cleanse him without sin, but only to purify polluted vessels. Christ, in me baptized, teaches me how to burn the thorns of sin ...

In effect, on the Eve of the Theophany, we witness religious dramatic writing at its most realistic and our particular veneration for St John the Baptist is explained. Is not he the chosen human instrument for this great Mystery? Hence we sing most solemnly:

You touched with your hand the pure Head of the Master.

The Baptism of Christ was an actual event, not to be repeated and unique in the course of history. But in blessing the water by his presence, Christ gave us, his Church, a blessed tradition: the blessing of holy water. At the Feast of the Theophany, it is customary for the officiating Priest and his congregation to find their way to the nearest source of water, be it river, sea or lake. Or, if this is not possible, then a large bowl of water in the church must suffice. And the Priest, and none other for this is a holy rite in the Name of Christ, after praying the prayers ordained, makes the sign of the Cross over the water three times and pronounces:

Therefore, O King, who loves mankind, be present now yourself as you were then through the descent of the Holy Spirit, and make this water holy.

Most solemnly, the Priest plunges the Cross into the water three times. The water thus sanctified is now truly ready to cleanse whatsoever it touches. Hence, the church is sprinkled, the faithful not only are sprinkled but also drink of the holy water. People are given water to take away, so that their homes too may be cleansed. Ikons may be washed carefully in this water, wounds tended, sick animals or poor pasture sprinkled. Holy water *is* holy; it is not a mirage, allegorical or symbolic:

Let us then draw water in gladness, O brethren: for upon those who draw with faith, the grace of the Spirit is invisibly bestowed by Christ the God and Saviour of our souls.

Perhaps a word on admission into the Orthodox

Church might be relevant here. Baptism, of course, is the key: the continued Feast of the Theophany. On one level, for the Orthodox, the Feast of the Theophany can be regarded as inaugurating what might be called 'official' Christianity. Without baptism, there can be no Christian. Christmas, the Nativity, saw the birth of Christ God. The Feast of the Meeting saw Christ God, in his humility, fulfilling the demands of the Old Law. The meeting with his people was the invitation for the Old to become the New. And now, the Old, on this Feast of the Theophany, is transformed into the New in the waters of the Jordan at his Baptism.

Admission into the Orthodox Church is by baptism in the Name of the Holy Trinity: the way blessed by God himself. And, here, perhaps a word of warning on over-done Orthodox rigour. We are, or should be, concerned with the one true baptism: baptism in the Name of the One Trinity *undivided*. And so we tend to get excited over the necessity to re-baptize some converts to the Orthodox faith. Re-baptism should only be necessary if the one intending to be Orthodox is convinced that he has not already been baptized in the Name of the Holy Trinity; otherwise, we are really transgressing in our zeal – no one should be subjected to being baptized twice.

In this connection it is good to remember that *anyone* can perform a baptism in a moment of crisis when no Priest is available. So to worry overmuch about Apostolic succession in preparing a candidate for admission into the Church is somewhat excessive – but, no doubt, on one level, typically Orthodox! We do tend to confuse nationality and language with Orthodoxy but that is a subject more suitable for consideration at Pentecost than the Feast of Christ's Baptism which speaks of the demand laid upon future Christians – a demand which is also a divine blessing.

And what of the water itself? Orthodoxy is a guard against any inclination to Pantheism whatever enticing form it may take because instead of ignoring forces potentially hostile to the Christian Faith, and instead of seeing such forces *as* enemies, following the precepts of divine love, Orthodoxy, at least in principle, excludes nothing from its embrace. We should not be in need of strange gods, or rites, or revelations, *outside* the Church.

The Church, in her loving generosity, makes use of each and all. Here, the water is blessed – and thereby taken into the innermost centre of our faith. Just as later, at the Feast of the Transfiguration, we shall see trees and fruit taken in, as it were, to play their part in cosmic worship of the One True God. The Old is ever fulfilled in the New, and as we celebrate the waters of the Jordan baptizing their God, the promise of this moment of glory was surely foreseen years before:

Call of the Lord above the waters,
The Lord above innumerable waters.
Call of the Lord in great might.
Call of the Lord in splendour. (Psalm 29:3–4)

The Transfiguration (6 August)

The history of salvation: Christ is born, Christ fulfils the Old Law; Christ inaugurates the New. And now, Christ manifests his divinity and draws into his divinity, into the New, into his unfailing love for *his* people, *his* Prophets who loved him from the beginning.

From the divine side, there is no break in the Tradition – only prejudice and stupidity on the human. In the first instance Christianity was meant for the chosen people of God, the Jews, in the second for the Gentiles. But, even as from the beginning some Jews actively denied him (some passively), and some were martyred for him, what are their heirs, the Gentiles, doing now? Or for that matter the Jews and all the other tangled races?

One important aspect of the Orthodox traditional worship is the abiding link with the Old Testament, the Prophets and the Psalms – all that went before and was treasured in memory and writing before the actual time of the Nativity. We never confuse the Old and New Testaments. Obviously, if we try to evaluate, they have not the same value, but it was not the Divine will to manifest himself other than to his own people even though some would betray him. And, this Feast of the Transfiguration emphasizes the continuity between Old and New.

The Feast of the Transfiguration, in particular, shows us not only the glory of Christ, Man truly God, but in the first place, demonstrates the extent of his love for us.

So often, we are torn with doubt. We long to see, we demand to witness, to hear, to touch, before ever we can begin to believe. And here, on Mount Tabor, he showed himself for who he was in truth: not merely a prophet, a teacher – but divine:

Before your Crucifixion, O Lord, the mountain became as heaven and a cloud spread itself out to form a tabernacle.

Such was his divine glory:

Your disciples, O Word, cast themselves down upon the ground, unable to gaze upon the Form that none may see.

They could not bear to look upon him and yet the Presence remained and they knew him for God.

It might well be asked why Christ chose to show himself in his divine glory only to three of his disciples. Why not at least to all the disciples? Why not to crowds? This divine vision – this 'sign' for which the people were always asking – why was it revealed only to three? And, if it comes to it, why only twelve apostles?

It would seem, yet again, that Christ refused proof to the people. Again and again he had the opportunity of convincing the crowds with some magnificent display of divinity – and he would not. Christ repeatedly taught the fallacy of numbers, the fallacy of facile popularity and, most insidious, spiritual *persuasion* of any kind. By his example, Christ taught us that our faith can only survive if it suffers doubt to the extreme point of human reason. God cannot be judged by his creatures on any system of results. We must survive on the most tenuous thread of proof – if it can be called proof: the indirect evidence of three of his disciples. We do not even know if the others believed their account of the vision: but *they* knew. They were the chosen three: Peter, James and John. Only three – and all three were men.

In his life on earth, Christ certainly did not ban women from his presence nor treat them with any suggestion of disdain – far from it. The women followed him in his journeys, they ministered to him and his disciples and they certainly were present at his crucifixion. Yet Christ only permitted his three disciples to be present at his Transfiguration. Why could women be at the Mystery of the Crucifixion but not at the Transfiguration? For us Orthodox, this 'contradiction' is not to be ignored. We see it as a direct command: only men – Priests – may enter the Holy Sanctuary and consecrate the wine and the bread. Only men were first permitted to witness Christ in his divine Transfiguration.

As women, there is much for us to do and much that we can do, but nowhere in the teaching or behaviour of Christ is there even a hint that we should overstep the line of the work we are blessed to do. Why should we need to? We are proud of being women. We will not allow any man to consider himself in the descent of the Most Holy Mother of God – why should we then seek what is not our heritage? The Mother of God is ever with us that we may rejoice *as* women – in being women:

Moses and Elijah saw upon Tabor God, who was made flesh of a virgin Maid for the redemption of mortal men.

No, the Old was never meant to be thrown out as an outworn garment when God became incarnate. We

57

retain the strong link with the Old, tending perhaps to over-emphasize the typological aspect.

Clearly it is possible to see the New prophesied in image in the Old, but the Old *does* live in its own right as well, and the Feast of the Transfiguration should remind us of this. Moses and Elijah were as much present as the three apostles. They represented the Old as *real* people – not images. 'They were counted worthy of this glory brighter than light.'

In some ways, the Feast of the Transfiguration is the most mysterious of the Feasts, at least on one level. It is dread-inspiring and overtly super-human. The baby was born, presented in the Temple and as a man baptized. It is true that the baptism was accompanied by strange signs for 'the heavens were opened unto him, and he saw the Spirit of God descending like a dove, and lighting upon him: And lo a voice from heaven, saying, "This is my beloved Son, in whom I am well pleased" ' (Matthew 3:16–17). Yet in the crowds and noise, the signs could have been missed or not fully understood. But here, at the Feast of the Transfiguration, there could be no doubt.

We are faced repeatedly in the text of the Feast with the bold impact of the event – and its challenge to our faith:

> *The leaders of the apostles went up with you into Mount Tabor, O Only-begotten Word most high, and Moses and Elijah were both present with you as attendants of God ...*

Mystery as *fact* – accept it:

> *On Tabor, O Christ, the glorious apostles recognized you as God and bent their knees before you in their amazement.*

The Feast of the Transfiguration comes in August – the time in Greece and further East for the grape harvest, and the time in Russia for the first apples. Traditionally, the Feast is associated with the offering of the first fruits – a lovely combination of the Divine and the human. We give our first fruits to God in the

58

tradition of the Old Testament, but Christ is God and so we confirm our faith in the Holy Trinity by the offering of our first fruits to Christ, transfigured on Mount Tabor.

When it comes to presenting our first fruits, it should not really be necessary to buy expensive imported grapes! Yet most of us are too conservative to bring our first summer cabbages to church! In fact, of course, the prayer of blessing refers to grapes specifically: '... bless the fruit of the vine lying here'.

However, in all seriousness, we return to the innermost meaning of the Transfiguration, not only in its unique realism – the demonstration of Christ's divinity – but also in how it spills over into the actuality of our daily lives as Christians. What does the Transfiguration bring to us in the world?

First and foremost the Transfiguration brings to us *the light* of eternal life: the light to which, as Christians, we are directing our daily lives. We are commanded to see the light, even if in terror we turn our backs and hide our eyes, and stop up our ears. The command is there and inexorable: not only must our individual light shine before men, but – a terrifying command – we must see this light in others.

The light was transferred upon humanity so palpably at this Feast of the Transfiguration. It was Christ as *man* who was transfigured on Mount Tabor. It was Christ as the Apostles knew him, and, as his disciples, we must recognize this light in others.

Transfiguration does not mean an idealistic attitude which can only lead to miserable disillusion – a romantic notion that there is some palpable good in everyone, that we can reform people, or manage to ignore their defects, or pretend in any way that bad is good. No. Transfiguration is infinitely more positive than all these evasions of reality. Surely it suggests not that bad is good or not as bad, but that we, in our faith, refuse to *yield* to the bad. We fix our eyes on the light of the transfigured Christ and somehow, within the Mystery, we take up the evil into ourselves. We love.

Of course we fail. As human beings, we can only love partially, not as God loves. Of course it does not really make sense on any rational or social level. The movement of the soul cannot be defined or explained or taught – but, somewhere it can work: the tiny grain of mustard seed. The secret shedding of light into the darkest places. We see the reality, we see the evil. And we love.

The reality of the Feast of the Transfiguration is a life-work which can never be accomplished: a life-work of unceasing prayer, of failure, of renewed work, of love. It is the turning of our backs on the seduction of evil, on darkness in its many forms. It is in every way the Feast of Light.

The seduction of evil is surely at its most inviting form in a rational approach to faith. How can you believe in a God of love when such dreadful things are allowed to happen? How? And, from such seductive questions we can, again and again, turn away and face the light which no evil can finally dim.

In *faith*, out of darkness, we walk into light but at the same time in *faith* we dare not approach. We hide our faces before the brilliance which sears the darkness within each of us.

The Feast of the Transfiguration is one of the strangest of the feasts, if I may put it like that, the most personally awesome, frightening even in its demands. The light shines in the darkness. The Uncreated momentarily appears within creation. Darkness and Light – ever in antithesis, but here, by the grace of God, momentarily one. 'And the darkness comprehended him not' (John 1:5).

The two hymns of the Feast, the *Apolytikion* and the *Kontakion*, both speak of the glory of Christ God and his infinite love in condescending to limit himself to human comprehension:

O Christ our God, you were transfigured on the mountain; you revealed your glory to your disciples in the measure of their power; so too may your light shine upon us, on *sinners, through the prayers of the Mother of God. Giver of Light, glory to you. (*Apolytikion, *Tone VII)*

*You were transfigured on the mountain and your disciples beheld your glory according to their measure, Christ God: so that, when they would see you crucified, they might know that your Passion was willed, and proclaim to the world that truly you are the radiance of the Father. (*Kontakion, *Tone VII)*

The Transfiguration reveals the love of Christ for his apostles – a personal, intimate love – and the intention of giving specifically to them the strength later to bear the separation of the crucifixion. Christianity, from the beginning, is not an impersonal religion: but the love of Love to the loved one.

The Transfiguration is ultimately the Feast of the *work* of love. In his Transfiguration, Christ was seen in his divine reality and his divinity – divinity hidden by his human body.

And should we not transfigure each other? Under our guise of good fellowship, charity, sweetness; under our guise of selfishness, cupidity, lust; under all the psychological and moral levels apparent to each other there lies the *reality*, known to God. Transfiguration means seeing the truth of ourselves and, as far as is possible, of each other, and – loving.

To love in the light of the Transfiguration is not making things easier by pretending that all and everyone are somehow better than common sense dictates. Transfiguration means reality and the demand of love, not idealism. The demand is to love Christ in his divinity – and man and ourselves, in our vileness.

Chapter 4

Feasts of Our Lord II

THE ENTRY INTO JERUSALEM
(Palm Sunday)
TO
PASCHA (Easter Sunday)

Palm Sunday

Christ – baptized, Christ – transfigured. Who is this who now enters Jerusalem seated upon an ass?

We have had many glimpses in the preceding Feasts, glimpses which have given us a sense not only of a transcendent Truth, but an immanent Reality. Now, as far as it is humanly possible, it seems as if we move into another dimension of this Reality: we move into being actual witnesses of the revelation of the fullness of God. It becomes a personal, awesome and exhilarating experience of participation.

On the *Sunday of Palms* we strew palms, haphazardly, recklessly, over the floors of our churches to be trodden on, taken home, treasured, discarded – even as the branches were strewn before Christ. In some mysterious way, our monastic, suburban, rural, urban church or cathedral *is* Jerusalem. *We* are Jerusalem: the stones, the mob, the children. For the moment it is all 'Hosanna!' Exciting and triumphant, who is this, as for the very first time, riding in on an ass? Is it a royal personage? Or a lowly one? Why is he here? Is it he whom the prophets foretold?

And we, through the texts which have survived over generations, can participate in the whole event: the triumph, the doubt, the praise and the foreboding of this Entry of Christ into Jerusalem – into our lives – for life or for death.

62

Great Vespers on the Saturday evening, the Vigil of the Feast, introduces the theme in its reality:

Today the grace of the Holy Spirit has gathered us together: and as we all take up your Cross we say: Blessed is he who comes, in the name of the Lord, Hosanna in the highest.

More explicitly:

He whose throne is Heaven, and the earth his footstool, Word of God the Father, and co-eternal Son, today has come into Bethany humbly, on an unreasoning foal ... let us also today, all the new Israel ... raise the triumphant shout: Hosanna in the highest, blessed is he who comes, King of Israel.

The Old and the New unite most emphatically at this Feast, so much prophecy, open and overt, is now fulfilled. This momentary triumphant resolution makes even more blindly cruel what is to come so soon. Now, wild excitement and triumph, but even at this moment arrangements must be made for the coming, the last, Passover. So little time now, and so much to be packed into a few days.

Six days before the Passover, Jesus came to Bethany, and his disciples came to him, saying to him, Lord, where do you wish that we make ready for you to eat the Passover ...?

The Old Testament readings in Great Vespers foretell what is now happening. Jacob's prophecy from Genesis, the Prophet Zephaniah, the Prophet Zechariah all pin-point the immediacy of the event.

Throughout Vespers, we are urged to grasp the immediacy of what is taking place. All is in the present tense, no legend: 'Behold your King comes in righteousness seated on an ass, exalted by children: Hosanna in the highest.' And again, 'The Saviour has come today to the city of Jerusalem, to fulfil the Scripture.'

The Vigil of Palm Sunday continues into Matins and the whole situation is repeated again and again so that

we, the faithful, may have it imprinted on mind and
heart:

> *The King of the Angels now has entered on a colt ... we*
> *cry to you: blessed is he who comes in the name of the*
> *Lord ... Today Christ enters the city of Bethany, sitting on a*
> *foal ... Today the grace of the Holy Spirit has gathered us*
> *together ...*

Another aspect of Orthodox spirituality is hinted at
here – the grace of the Spirit has brought us to church.
It is a privilege, a gift of God, to be allowed to take part
in worship. It is not a duty, nor a praiseworthy act on
our part! It remains an inestimable privilege to be
allowed to participate in a Feast in the presence of the
whole heavenly communion.

Throughout the Vigil Service, we are constantly
reminded of the peculiar nature of the Feast. Again
and again we hear the same theme conveyed in
various texts: 'On this day, the Sunday of Palms, we
celebrate the radiant and glorious feast of the entry
into Jerusalem of our Lord Jesus Christ.' His entry
into Jerusalem – and our entry with him into his
agony, his death, his resurrection.

Holy Week

The First Three Days
When we go into Holy Week, on the evening of Palm
Sunday, it always seems as if we will never come out of
it, that it is impossible for the Sunday of the
Resurrection ever to dawn for us very early in the
morning.

How can it be possible? How *is* it possible? One short
week: a King, a man, God rides into Jerusalem – and
on the very next Sunday, Christ God rises from the
dead. The Day of Resurrection. Seven days. The whole
salvation of mankind is accomplished. The actual
body; the crucified body; the resurrected body – within

the compass of a few days. From hour to hour we live them and each day of Holy Week is precious for its peculiar significance.

On the Monday, Tuesday and Wednesday we are preparing for the crucifixion. To a certain extent we are still connected with the normal reality of life in as much as the offices are as they have been throughout the Great Fast and the psalms are read at their regular times. But these three days are marked out by their special hymn at Matins, a hymn which has come to represent the whole service for many of the Orthodox – Greek or Russian or Arabic or whosoever they might be. This is the Hymn (*Troparion*) of the Bridegroom. The hymn is the stern warning for us all as we embark on Holy Week: to be alive, awake, alert: not only physical but spiritual apathy may cause banishment from the heavenly kingdom, banishment which is damnation.

The hymn invites us to repent at this very last possible minute. It reminds us that Christ is not a religion, but a Person: a King who has just ridden into our city. He may be out of our sight at this present moment but he can demand admission at his own will; he is the Bridegroom and we all are his servants – attendants upon his bridal chamber. It is for us to be alert and keep our lamps lit at whatever cost of weariness and despondency. The penalty of banishment if we cease to keep vigil for his coming is infinitely worse than any temporary discomfort, pain – even martyrdom.

The rubric for the Hymn reads: 'We sing the *Troparion* slowly and audibly and with sweet melody' – *audibly*: not mumbled to ourselves but for all to hear, and in Tone VIII, the tone to take us out of this world.

Behold the Bridegroom comes in the middle of the night: and blessed is the servant whom he finds watching: but unworthy he whom he finds heedless. See to it, then, my soul, not to be weighed down by sleep, lest you be handed over to death and shut out from the kingdom: but rouse yourself crying: Holy, Holy, Holy is God: through the prayers of the Mother of God, have mercy upon us.

This hymn marks the opening of Matins for us in the first three days of Holy Week, but, as familiar and significant is the *Exapostilarion*, the hymn preceding the daily Lauds psalms.

Again, the image is that of the bridal chamber, but now it is the memory of the man cast out because he was not wearing a wedding garment. In a parish church, the cantor may stand in the middle of the church to sing this traditional plea for compassion with its haunting melody – a plea and a confession of faith even as we confess our inadequacy:

Your bridal chamber I see adorned, O my Saviour, and I have not the garment that I may enter in: O give light to the raiment of my soul, Giver of Light, and save me.

We stand there in the knowledge of our souls darkened from sin and, equally, in the knowledge of salvation. Salvation and damnation both equally real. A Mystery.

In these first three days of Holy Week we continue to pray the prayer of St Ephraim which we have been praying throughout the Great Lent, and we continue to recite the psalms. These first three days still link us to the reality of the Great Lent which has gone before, but at the same time, they prepare us for the plunge into the isolated, naked, relentless tide of events leading into the crucifixion. All the familiar landmarks of the services are swept away, even the basis of the psalms:

The upper room was laid ready and received you, the Creator, with your initiated, and there you kept the Passover and enacted its Mysteries.

Each of the last days has its own chronologically real significance.

Holy Thursday

Thursday – the day of the Last Supper, the institution

of Holy Communion and the blessing to Judas to do what he would do.

Of your mysterious supper, Son of God, today admit me a partaker. For I will not speak of the mystery to your enemies, nor give you a kiss as Judas, but as the thief I will confess you. Remember me, Lord, when you come into your kingdom.

This hymn is sung repeatedly, taking the place of others normally sung in the Liturgy throughout the year.

Repeatedly we hear of the treachery. It was a real betrayal, not a theological concept: '... he hurried to sell the one without price'. We compare Judas with the harlot who poured out her love in sweet ointment:

O wretchedness of Judas! To see the harlot kissing the footprints and cunningly to devise betrayal with a kiss: she loosed her hair, but he entangled himself in passion, carrying foul-smelling malice instead of myrrh ...

Inexorably the time went on in Jerusalem, and inexorably the time goes on now, Holy Week after Holy Week, in every Orthodox church. And we have come to Thursday night: the time appointed for Matins of Holy Friday, the Matins of the Twelve Gospels. The faithful gather in churches, monasteries and cathedrals for the celebration of the Twelve Gospels, even, perhaps unconsciously, because they do not wish to miss the *event*. It is not a question of the celebration of a service, however reverently commemorative. Time is irrelevant, it is the re-living in spirit of the Passion, *here* and *now*. How dare we not be present? How can we bear to miss the terror, the cruelty, the self-condemnation – and the hope?

Year after year, we experience the celebration of the Twelve Gospels as something dearly familiar, and something new. Within the measure of time it seems to happen every year as if it had never happened previously. A logical nonsense, a spiritual reality.

We gather in church. We hold our candles, alight for each reading of the Gospel. The Gospel lies in the middle of the church, ready for the Priest to read the Passion. The choir will sing the verses in between the Readings. The Deacon will cense with the sweet fragrance of the funeral spices. This is the Matins of the Twelve Gospels:

The first reading is the longest: John 13:31 – 18:1. At its completion we sing, as we do after each of the subsequent Gospels: 'Glory to your long-suffering, O Lord, glory to you.'

Between the Gospels come the Antiphons, each one, again and again impressing upon us the reality of what *is* happening now. This is not simply an historical event.

Judas ran to the lawless scribes and said: 'What will you give me if I will betray him to you?' But even as they were bargaining about you, you stood amongst them yourself unseen by them who were doing the bargaining. O you, who know the heart, spare our souls.

Our souls: we should never see ourselves as the virtuous onlooker or objective historian.

More uncompromising is the reiteration of Judas's consciousness of what he was about to do – 'But lawless Judas did not wish to understand.' Judas's deliberate blindness becomes the warning for us: 'Watch and pray, that you are not tempted, you said to your disciples, Christ our God'.

Long-suffering: this divine attribute comes repeatedly during the Matins of the Twelve Gospels. Long-suffering, omniscient and divine Love:

When you fed the disciples at the supper, you knew the plan for the betrayal, and you chose Judas for it: you knew that he was incorrigible, and you wished everyone to understand that you were betrayed of your own will in order to snatch the world out of the grasp of the enemy: O long-suffering, glory to you.

68

Long-suffering? Christ is surely not only long-suffering during the Passion, the trial and the Crucifixion; he is long-suffering while still in various forms we continue to betray him, each one of us in our own individual way.

The second reading is: John 18:1–28. Once again comes the inexorable *today*:

> *Today Judas forsakes the Master, and takes the devil to himself: he is blinded by passion for money, and in darkness falls away from the light ...*

In the verses that follow, we cannot escape the horror of this betrayal: '... he sells the Lord for thirty pieces of silver; with a treacherous kiss he betrays him to death ...' The reality of the event is sustained by lack of commentary. We are subjected to the stark reality of the event with no relief: 'Today they pierced his side with a sword who scourged Egypt with plagues for their sake ...' But it is ever *his* 'willed' Passion: God cannot be a human victim.

One of the most poignant moments of the service comes in the reproach to Judas. Judas was a *real* man, a man numbered among Christ's friends, trusted as the others. How *could* he betray the Master who loved him even as he loved the other disciples? The reproach, sung by a single voice, carries all the grief of the betrayal:

> *What was there, Judas, in his behaviour to make you betray the Saviour? Did he cut you off from the company of the apostles? Did he deprive you of the grace of healing? Did he turn you away from the table when you were at supper with the others? When he washed the others' feet, did he scorn yours?*

In meditating upon the Matins of the Twelve Gospels, it seems impossible to convey the fullness of the experience without writing out the whole service – but even that would not suffice. Such is the realism of Orthodox worship, it becomes essential to be present – no recital of events or quotation of passages can begin to be adequate to the actual participation in the event.

Perhaps the most striking characteristic of the whole service is the intensity of repetition: every nail of the Cross seems driven into us, and throughout the repeated experience of Christ's *actual* suffering, there runs the thread of self-accusation – which of us can exclude the Judas from ourselves?

They, the loyal apostles, Judas the betrayer, the crowds – they were *all* Jews. Some actively betrayed, some indifferently, a very few remained faithful. Supposedly, we are *all* Christians – what can we say for ourselves?

Thrice Peter denied and at once understood what had been said to him, but he brought you tears of repentance: O God be merciful to me and save me.

Inexorably, the service continues, and there is no escape from the horror:

Today he is hung upon the tree who hung the earth upon the waters. A crown of thorns is put on him who is King of the Angels. He is clothed in false purple who clothes the sky with clouds. He accepts blows in the face who set Adam free in the Jordan. The Bridegroom of the Church is fast fixed with nails. The Son of the Virgin is pierced with a spear. We bow down before your Passion O Christ'. (3 times)

And yet there is light in the darkness: 'Show us also your glorious Resurrection.' Crucifixion and Resurrection are bound close in Mystery.

Holy Friday

On the Friday of Holy Week, the Liturgy is never celebrated. Our concentration is on the crucifixion. Because we feel ourselves present at the foot of the Cross, we abstain from food during the whole day. This is not any form of penance, nor duty, but simply that we do not wish to eat when our God is being crucified before our eyes. Our rejoicing at the Resurrection, in effect, will be equally spontaneous. Crucifixion and resurrection remain for us actual events on the days on which they are celebrated, and we feel on those days as if we are being allowed to participate in events unlimited by time and yet totally real. Time is eliminated in the inspiration of the services.

In the morning of Holy Friday the Royal Hours are celebrated, and in the afternoon, Vespers. It is during Vespers that the full reality of the crucifixion comes upon the Orthodox faithful. At the end of the service, the *Apolytikion* (hymn) is sung in Tone II (the tone of mourning) in which there is no hint of the triumph to come. At this hour it is the wail of the dirge. The shroud is carried in procession to be placed in the middle of the church. It is a real shroud, sometimes decked in flowers, and it is brought as to the place of burial. Joseph of Arimathaea has claimed the body, and he takes it to the new tomb. Here the service breaks off – the actual Service of the Entombment will follow later in Matins, normally celebrated on Friday night.

Noble Joseph took your pure body down from the tree, and when he had wrapped it in clean linen with sweet spices, he laid and enclosed it within a new tomb.

Holy Saturday

At the end of Matins of Holy Saturday, the burial procession is completed. The faithful strew flowers on the shroud in image of the sweet spices cast by the women because it was the Sabbath and they could not tend the body with the customary preparatory rites for burial.

Matins ends, but many of the faithful remain to keep watch by the body of their Lord. It is our tribute to our Master, whose Ikon lies crucified before us in

71

the middle of his church. And, even as we do for our own dead, while we watch, we read the psalms.

Holy Saturday dawns. The readings from the Old Testament bring first promise: – a promise for the future which is now upon us. The Liturgy of St Basil is celebrated. Today sees the removal of all the black vestments which have draped the church. And yet it hardly seems possible that we are really emerging from the Great Lent and the stark desolation of Holy Week.

Can we really ever be excited and spiritually *warm* again? Can we feast and make merry? Surely we have neither the strength nor the desire. But if we feel like this, what must the eleven have felt and the faithful women?

Midnight approaches. Christ is crucified. He is dead and buried. The shroud is strewn with flowers. He has left us.

Pascha

Crowds begin to gather. The church is dark. Why are we here? And – suddenly – the world performs a somersault! Death? But, Death *is* Life. Resurrection is not possible without Crucifixion.

Out of the darkness of the church we follow the procession of flickering candles. We are the women coming to the tomb. The tomb is empty! There is no body! Our voices rise again and again as we process round the church, we are singing the angelic hymn of victory over all the forces of darkness – over unbelief, desecration and heresy – the hymn that has been sung from generation to generation in Tone VI – traditional, triumphant, majestic. Our voices rise to heaven – discordant they may be, out of tune and blown away by the wind, but we sing the *truth*! And we *believe*, *today*:

Your resurrection O Christ Saviour angels are singing in the heavens, and on earth make us worthy with pure hearts to glorify you.

Greek, Arabic, Slavonic or English – what does it matter? All the Orthodox are singing the same words of glory all over the world. And this is only the beginning of the celebration of the reality of Pascha.

And the church? It is indeed a transfigured church: white, golden, lights blazing, radiant vestments and doors wide open even into the altar for at this moment no barrier is permitted between earth and heaven. No more repentance even for this blessed hour – no bows, no prostrations, no kneeling. It is the resurrection. Christ *is* risen.

This is no normal service. It is a royal function. The human greeting is to the King of kings. Throughout the service that follows, the cry is repeated, 'Christ is risen!', and full-throated comes the reply from the assembled people, 'He is risen indeed'.

In countries such as ours, where frequently the congregation is of mixed origin, each group is determined to out-cry its neighbour, 'He is risen indeed' – in English, in Greek and Slavonic! Enthusiastically we out-cry our fellow faithful while the censing Priest achieves a great feat of memory in using the appropriate language to each group in his evoking cry: 'Christ is risen!' The howl of 'Crucify him', 'Let him be crucified' is transformed into this one glorious acclamation: 'He is risen indeed.'

'Stand upright'; be vigilant my soul. Can not this crowd so smoothly slip back, revert, turn the rejoicing to sneers and blows and spitting? But, surely, at least not for these few hours of rejoicing?

The Ikon of the Resurrection is venerated. The Easter kiss is exchanged: the threefold kiss of Pascha in which we confess the Trinity. And then comes the reading of the homily of St John Chrysostom. This homily is one of the loveliest in our possession. It is tender and forgiving as is only proper at such a moment of Divine Love. It is the invitation to Holy Communion for all the Orthodox, irrespective of their conscious preparation and overlooking, as only Christ himself could, canonical conditions. For once, in the presence of the Risen Christ, we can freely enjoy his generosity:

> *If any have laboured from the first hour let him today receive his due payment. If any have come after the third hour let him feast gratefully. And he that arrived only after the sixth hour let him in no wise hesitate for he too shall suffer no loss. And if any have delayed to the ninth hour let him approach also without hesitation.*

The divine invitation to Holy Communion is the most glorious moment of a glorious service:

> *Let no one lament his transgressions, for forgiveness has risen from the tomb ... Hell was embittered when it met you below: it was embittered for it is made void: it was embittered for it is mocked: embittered for it has been slain ... O Hell, where is your victory? Christ is risen and you are laid low. Christ is risen, and the demons have fallen. Christ is risen ...*

What rhetoric! St John Chrysostom was indeed a great preacher!

If the Orthodox can fast, we know how to feast as well! The Easter Vigil – the Liturgy – is followed by the Easter Feast, a true break-fast! At this point each country has its native custom for the 'correct' food. We can be as pedantic over our Paschal Feast as we were over our Fast!

For the Russians, no Paschal Feast is worthy of respect unless the festal board boasts *kulitch* and *pascha*! *Kulitch* is a pillar of sweet bread and *pascha* a geometric shape formed primarily of *tvorog* (cheese made of soured milk essentially), eggs and *smetana* (not yoghourt but akin). In fact, its recipe is unbelievably complicated and its taste unbelievably delicious. There is also every kind of sausage. There are hams and pies. And of course eggs – eggs in all colours and designs.

The Feasting is not limited to one day. The week of suffering, of darkness, now becomes the week of light – the week of joy.

Palm Sunday to Pascha is a journey of prayer, of immediate experience. Perfect Man, Perfect God – and now, until the Ascension, the Risen Christ.

Chapter 5

Feasts of Our Lord III

THE ASCENSION AND AFTER

The Feast of the Ascension

For forty days during the Great Fast of Lent we wandered in the wilderness. Our comfort came from the Old Testament prophets who in their loneliness knew in their very being that the Messiah would come; the prophets, who in the face of adversity, mockery, persecution and exile, still looked up to heaven in unshaken faith.

For forty days we were deprived of the food of life: no Liturgies during the week; no readings from the Gospels; for forty days we knew what it was to live without the presence of Christ, our God – but we also knew that the forty days would end. The Light was shining far ahead. We were on a journey of loneliness and finally of agony, but the Light was at the end.

And now? Where is this Light? Yes, Christ has risen and walks beside us for forty days. We are no longer in the wilderness only made bearable by faith. We have put our hands into his side. Faith, for the time being, is linked with actual experience. But the Christ we knew during the years of his active life on earth is no longer with us. This Christ is, as it were, elusive. We meet him unexpectedly, he invites us to eat with him; we hardly dare believe who he is. Such are these forty days on earth.

But the time is at hand for the fullness of his divinity to be revealed to us: the reality of Christ, Perfect Man and Perfect God. We have lived with him as Man, we have seen him resurrected in the body. Years before we knew him to be Divine at his baptism.

Man/God has always been present in every form of manifestation. And now?

Is the moment of ascension one of glory or desolation? He came down into the womb of his human Mother – and now he returns into the very being of his heavenly Father. Are we to rejoice at this final manifestation of divinity? Or are we to weep because he is leaving? It is surely a Feast of mingled joy and sorrow:

> *The apostles, seeing you taken up into the clouds, filled with sorrow, cried through their tears: O Master do not leave us orphans and alone, your servants, whom you tenderly loved, but send to us, as you promised, the Holy Spirit, guide and enlightener of our souls.*

The whole Ascension Service is permeated with this double movement of joy and sorrow: how can we not mourn his departure? How can we not fear? And, how can we not rejoice in this further sign of his divinity?

The Ascension is a Feast unique for this resolution of opposites. It is also unique for the witnessing of faith actually based on knowledge, on what the apostles had *seen*. Now, left alone, they could continue to act in faith but they retained the living memory.

At this Feast we are with the apostles on the Mount of Olives:

> *And we, O Master, who share in that joy of your going back to heaven, give glory to your great mercy which has come to us.*

We *share*. Once again, the Feast is not an expression of doctrine, but an event outside time in which we *share*. Christ ascends to his heavenly home and with tears and joy we see him go. But he will come again even as he has promised: 'In the same way as you have seen Christ going up, he will come again in the flesh, the righteous judge of all.'

It is all of a piece, from the radiant promise at Christmas, the desolation of the crucifixion, the revelation of the resurrection, to this moment of the ascension:

*As they saw you, our Saviour, one body with us, borne into
the heights, the heavenly powers proclaimed: O Master and
Lord, great is your love of man!*

We need only go to the texts of our services for our
confession of faith. What could be more explicit than
the final prayer of Ascension Matins? It sums up what
has been and it prepares us for what is about to come –
Pentecost:

*You were born as you yourself willed, you appeared as you
yourself proposed: our God, you suffered in the flesh: you
rose from the dead, having trampled down death, and were
received up into glory, and so fulfilled all things.*

And now comes the promise:

*... and you sent to us the divine Spirit to praise and glorify
your divinity.*

The Feast of Pentecost

It is significant that for the Orthodox Pentecost is the
Feast of the Holy Trinity. We do not separate them into
event and doctrine. At Pentecost we experience the
manifestation of the Holy Spirit and that is the Feast.
The Father we have known from the beginning; the
Son has appeared to us in the flesh and returned to the
Father; and now the Spirit descends upon the Church.
    When we pray to the Spirit to abide in us, when we
worship the Spirit as the Third Person of the Trinity,
when we think of the work of the Spirit, it seems as if
our Orthodox approach fundamentally differs from
that of many of our fellow Christians, and it differs in
a way significant to our whole attitude to the faith.
    The Spirit came down upon the Church at Pentecost.
For us, that is the work of the Spirit: to keep the
teaching of the Church, the living awareness of the
Truth in us, not to set new fashions in belief. We pray
for the inspiration of the Spirit for fear lest without his

78

help we will lose the continuity, be set adrift and sink in contrary waves of contemporary thought. The Spirit ever illumines what *is* – not what was, or what might be. Repeatedly we pray: 'O holy One, visit and heal our infirmities.'

The Spirit comforts: he strengthens, heals and inspires. Without the Spirit we could not recognize the Father, nor the Son: baptism is in the Name of the *Trinity*:

> *King of Heaven, Comforter, Spirit of truth, everywhere present and filling all things, treasure of blessings, and giver of life, come and abide in us, cleanse us from all corruption, and of your goodness, save our souls.*

The Spirit came upon the Church, and all spoke in strange languages. Hence, it has been the Orthodox tradition that if a country becomes Orthodox, all the liturgical books should forthwith be translated into the native language. When Russia was converted to Christianity, immediately all the Greek books were translated into Slavonic.

There have been many individual efforts to translate into English, but of course there is no traditional necessity since England is not an Orthodox country. Even so, the disinclination for translation, even among some of the converts to Orthodoxy, is somewhat surprising *vis à vis* our devotion to Pentecost as a Feast! It is worth considering perhaps what some of the apostles must have felt when they heard Christ's own words – which they had personally heard – translated into some barbaric tongue! But they did not protest. And we, in our liturgical texts, delight in this revelation of the Spirit, whilst we deny it in practice:

> *When you sent down your Spirit, O Lord, to the waiting apostles, the children of the Hebrews, seeing them, were beside themselves with amazement, for they heard them speaking in strange tongues as the Spirit gave them utterance ...*

But this does not mean that we continue to translate and re-translate familiar and beloved texts. The Spirit is not the Creator of fashion or agitation. He establishes our wavering feet in the true faith – he does not seduce them into fanciful sidesteps.

The Devil takes many shapes, but perhaps his favourite mask in our time is that of the Spirit. He seeks to shake the very foundation of the Christian faith by the persuasive presentation of 'seeking', 'searching', of putting human feelings, human ambition, human satisfaction and self-satisfaction before all else.

We must be careful when the Spirit leads us away from the road of the Cross; when the Spirit offers us success, even spiritual success or satisfaction; when the Spirit whispers to us that it is right for us to seek what pleases us; when the Spirit leads us in the direction of willed self-fulfilment (whatever that might be) – in effect, when the Spirit tells us that we need not suffer. Then we should stop, as at a glaring red light. This is *not* the Spirit.

The true Spirit, the Spirit of Truth, the Spirit of Life, leads us into the wilderness of doubt, temptation and desolation, and demands the faith which alone is the answer to doubt. Pentecost is the Feast of the true Spirit, 'to believers an agent of salvation'. Without the Spirit, Christ remains a divine figure, a Sunday observance – but not a living God with us now as he was in Galilee:

> *Tongues were once confused through the presumption which built the tower: but now tongues are made wise through the glory of the knowledge of God. Then God condemned the impious for their offence, now Christ enlightens the fishermen with the Spirit. Then was imposed discord of tongues for punishment, now is restored harmonious concord of many tongues for the salvation of our souls.*

Tower of Babel and Pentecost. These are not to be confused. But the only safeguard is the knowledge of the presence of the Spirit. Without the Spirit, our prayers in congregation or alone may well be Babel. We must always pray for the presence of the Spirit, lest we fall into confusion:

Come near to us, come near, you who are everywhere: even as you are always with your apostles, so unite yourself to those yearning for you, O Compassionate One: that united we may sing you, and glorify your all-holy Spirit.

Whenever we are tempted either to forget the Holy Spirit or see him as an excuse for changing that which requires no human change, we might remember this verse of Pentecost Lauds:

The Holy Spirit ever was and is and shall be, with neither beginning nor end, but eternally ranked with the Father and the Son.

The Spirit's work is to keep the Faith ever alive – in its eternal principle:

Through him the Father is known and the Son is glorified and all come to know one Power, one Order, one worship of the Holy Trinity.

So we come to the end of eleven of the Great Feasts of the Church – Feasts which contain and expound our faith: our journey of prayer, praise and supplication; our confession of the real event.

But, the twelfth of the Feasts has a peculiar character of its own for it is not from within the Gospels but derives directly from the actual fact of the crucifixion.

The Feast of the Exaltation of the Cross (14 September)

A Feast on its own and a strange Feast: it is a Feast; yet it is a Feast on which we fast. How can a Feast be a Fast? Yet, how could we feast in the face of the Cross? Its full title is: the Feast of the Exaltation of the Precious and Life-giving Cross.

An interesting way to approach this Feast might well be by way of the story of St Mary of Egypt. St Mary – a harlot of Egypt from the time she was a mere child – was only remarkable for the fact that she sold her body but would never solicit or even accept money for her prostitution. But she lusted generously – avidly.

St Mary haunted the market-place and fed on the daintiest food which Egypt and her lovers could provide – yet she worked with her hands, spinning that she might earn what she needed to sustain life. Never satisfied with the men she might entice, St Mary always went on searching, searching for something she did not, and could not, realize in her imagination. She only knew that she must go on – she *must*.

One day she followed a group of attractive young men on to a boat. She was intent on corrupting them to the best of her ability and they offered no objection to free entertainment. She heard that they were on their way to Jerusalem to celebrate the Feast of the Exaltation of the True Cross. This meant nothing to her, but the prospect of the voyage in their company meant a great deal. In fact, she spent the journey in seducing as many of the young men as she possibly could.

On reaching Jerusalem, with no comprehension of what she was doing, she followed the crowds to the church on the holy day of the Elevation of the Cross – the one day in the year when the Cross was brought out to be seen and venerated by the people:

> *With great labour and effort I, poor wretch, squeezed myself right up to the very doors of the church at which the crowd would be shown the life-giving tree. But when I stepped on to the threshold of the doors, over which everyone else was freely going in, some kind of power held me back ...*

This was the true Cross, brought out to the people on the Feast for veneration. St Mary was pushed back until a mighty wave of repentance filled her whole being. She prayed before the Ikon of the Mother of God and she was allowed to see the Cross. Then, led by a divine Power, she disappeared into the desert wilderness where miraculously she survived, unseen to all until her last meeting in this world with the Priest-Monk Zossima.

The Cross destroyed her; the Cross brought her to life. Her body withered; her soul lived.

The Feast of the Cross comes after the resurrection, after Pentecost. It is a Feast directly concerned with the living of our lives here and now; it signifies the presence of all that Christ taught us – and all that Christ did on earth to save our souls. Christ has ascended into heaven but his Cross survives on earth. We take up our crosses in everything we do. *The* Cross is made up of an infinite number of little crosses – one for each individual Christian, bestowed at baptism and carried until death.

The Cross for the Orthodox, in our worship, is as ever wholly real and is never divorced from the resurrection. The Cross is full of indescribable agony – the agony of Christ – for those who loved him and witnessed his death, but its significance never stops at this point. Even as we do not venerate the Mother of God without her Son, so we do not adore her Son's crucifixion without his resurrection. The Cross without the resurrection has no meaning; in fact, it is worse than having no meaning for it suggests a cruel God, or a God who imposes agony as a prerequisite for sanctity – pain and torment in a senseless context.

We carry our little crosses into a light of glory; we are not told to cling to them as if pain is good in itself. Christ relieves pain. He heals. The Cross of Christ overcame death once and for all – death in all its forms. Actual death – for he rose on the third day, but also every other death. The Cross overcomes the death of love, the death of the spirit, the death of the individual soul.

If we fix ourselves on the Cross, we free ourselves from the slavery to the world. We die to the seduction of the world and rise emancipated, truly laying aside 'all the cares of this life'. The price may seem too heavy – death to the luxury of Egypt's fish and wine. Can it be too heavy? On the Cross we are set free: we need no longer compete with our fellow beings, yearn for new furniture or envy our neighbour's latest car. At the Liturgy we sing:

Before your Cross, we bow down in worship, O Lord, and your holy resurrection we glorify.

Your Cross – and all that signifies now – and for ever.

O you, raised up on the Cross of your own will, Christ God, grant your compassion to your new state, of the same name as you. Gladden our faithful kings in your power, granting victory to them over their enemies. They have your support, the weapon of peace, invincible victory. (The *Kontakion* at the Feast)

The tradition of the psalms persists: the God of Israel is now our God – whom we ask unashamedly to lead us into victory over our enemies. I should like to think that most of us now consider these enemies as the vicious thoughts of our hearts, but I am not only not convinced of such altruism but also I am not sure that we should totally emasculate all our prayers for help against those who assault us. Perhaps, we should be more honest with ourselves at least in prayer. Our English traditional tendency is to water down as much as is possible to avoid offence in any direction: where the whole Catholic and Orthodox world may quite happily exclaim 'My God!' in a diversity of languages, English substitutes 'Good gracious' or 'Good heavens' or any other euphemism pleasing to the Puritan tradition.

The Cross is the salvation of mankind, in image

identified with the tree of the forbidden fruit. A tree cast us out of Paradise, a tree once again opens its gates:

It was fitting that wood should be healed by wood.

Perhaps most emphatic of all comes the singing of the *Exapostilarion* (the hymn sung after the Canon of the day at Matins):

The Cross is the guardian of the whole earth; the Cross is the beauty of the Church. The Cross is the strength of kings; the Cross is the support of the faithful. The Cross is the glory of the angels and the wounder of demons.

What else, after this, can there be left to say? All that is left for us is simply to venerate the Cross. If we no longer possess even one particle of the true Cross, it does not matter: the sanctity flows from blessing to blessing, generation to generation, true Cross to our little cross.

And there it lies upon a tray, adorned with branches of basil or fragrant flowers – the everlasting memory of the strewn spices upon the beloved body. It is brought in procession from out of the sanctuary and placed in the middle of the church, on a table specially prepared. The ceremony of the elevation of the cross is deeply solemn, with the *Lord, have mercy* sung five hundred times, a hundred times at each elevation. The cross remains in the centre of the church, to be venerated, to be the presence of our salvation, until the last day of the Feast, 21 September.

When Jesus therefore saw his mother, and the disciple standing by, whom he loved, he saith unto his mother, Woman, behold thy son! Then saith he to the disciple, Behold thy mother! And from that hour that disciple took her unto his own home.

Thus was blessed the union between us and the Mother of God: we take her into our homes, she is our Mother.

'But when they came to Jesus, and saw that he was dead already ...' Without his death there could have been no Resurrection. Death could not be overcome without death. The Cross for us is life. Without the true death on the real Cross there could be no true resurrection. And we see the Cross and the resurrection not as theology but as *reality*.

The Cross and the resurrection trample down death: every form of death, above all, actual death. Death has no more dominion. With the Cross before us, courage is given to trample down other aspects of death – sin, our own personal sin. Sin is death – the Cross is life.

The Cross was the door into life for St Mary of Egypt and it remains our door. The Cross once crucified Christ God, but in his life eternal it crucifies sin, evil, hatred. The Cross is triumphant. Glory to the Cross:

The Cross is the guardian of the whole earth; the Cross is the beauty of the Church. The Cross is the strength of kings; the Cross is the support of the faithful. The Cross is the glory of the angels and the wounder of demons.

All the ends of the earth give glory, all the devils are affrighted. How great a gift is here bestowed on mortal men! Through your Cross, save our souls, O Christ, you who alone are full of compassion.

Chapter 6

Prayers of the Heart

All the prayers of the Feasts and the Fasts in the Services of the Church have been communal prayers of the faithful people: they have expressed the doctrine of the Church, they have expressed worship and veneration and they have marked out days and seasons for the Christian. But there are two prayers which are peculiarly individual – the prayer of St Ephraim, still vocal, and, ultimately, the Jesus Prayer, the silent prayer of the heart.

The Ephraim Prayer

O Lord and Master of my life, give me not a slothful spirit, meddlesome, lustful of power, and vain of word. (full prostration)

But a spirit sober, humble, patient, and loving, grant to me, your servant. (full prostration)

Yea, O Lord King, grant me to see my own transgressions, and not to judge my brother, for you are blessed unto the ages of ages. Amen. (full prostration)

O God cleanse me a sinner. (12 times, bow to the ground)

O Lord and Master of my life, give me not a slothful spirit, meddlesome, lustful of power, and vain of word. But a spirit sober, humble, patient, and loving, grant to me, your servant. Yea, O Lord King, grant me to see my own transgressions, and not to judge my brother, for you are blessed unto the ages of ages. Amen. (full prostration)

This prayer accompanies us throughout the whole of the Great Lent. It is said at the conclusion of all the daily services but not on Sunday – Sunday is ever the day of Resurrection, and stands out from any other day throughout the whole year.

The Ephraim Prayer of course is fundamentally a monastic prayer, applicable to the monk in his daily routine, in his life within a community and all the spiritual and moral niceties of such a life. But that is no reason why it cannot be made applicable to us all – within our families, or even at work. It is the true prayer of self-evaluation, of repentance, and the prayer of the plea for help.

The Ephraim Prayer is strikingly representative of the deeply fundamental Orthodox attitude to sin and repentance. Here, specific sin is mentioned, but specific in the widest category of classification: we *are* sinful. As fallen man we cannot be but sinful. Hence our repentance is ever an attitude of the spirit. Our personal sins, peculiar to ourselves and our lives, are matters for confession and absolution: but, our *sin* – the sin of fallen man – is ever with us. We can only throw ourselves again and again at the feet of the merciful God and cry out for forgiveness.

In effect, we *are* sinners. Sin has taken its dwelling in us but we do not despair. Christ, in tender compassion, looks down on us from the Cross, and opens the gates of Paradise to the repentant thief.

The Jesus Prayer

So much has been talked and written about the Jesus Prayer in recent years that perhaps it might be of some importance to explain quite simply its essential nature. Above all, of course, the Jesus Prayer is not an esoteric exercise, nor, in its true meaning, can it have any significance for the non-Christian.

The Jesus Prayer is the *Jesus* prayer. It is not the medium for any form of floating away from the troubles of the world, nor of meditation for the sake of meditation, nor indeed anything which is not a purely

Christian and, on one level, *practical* form of prayer. The Jesus Prayer: a life-work for a Christian.

The words of the prayer are:

Lord, Jesus Christ, Son of God, have mercy upon me, a sinner.

If we analyse this sentence into each vital part, where do we arrive on our spiritual road?

Lord Master, one to whom we owe our duty on every level. If he is Lord, then we are subject to him. *Lord* – our Master, in the world and in heaven. This opening word is a self-dedication and acknowledgment of inferiority. *Lord* – we bow down before him. We treat him, and all that appertains to him, with the greatest reverence. He is *Lord* – God Almighty in heaven and upon earth.

Jesus His name. True God and true Man. His was a real birth. 'And when eight days were accomplished for the circumcising of the child, his name was called Jesus, which was so named of the angel before he was conceived in the womb' (Luke 2:21). A real baby and a real name, but not without divine connotation – the name was decreed by God's heavenly messenger.

Christ The Saviour. God Incarnate. God, taking flesh upon himself to save his people. The whole history of salvation from birth, through crucifixion – to resurrection – the overcoming of death. They rose from the tombs; they will rise. The gates of Paradise are reopened. No more the flaming sword. Christ so long awaited, Christ rejected, scorned, crucified. Christ: the climax – Lord, Jesus Christ.

Son of God Paradox. He *is* God – the Second Person of the Trinity: he *is* the Son of God. In the limitation of the human mind we cannot untangle the divine Mystery but we can believe and trust in the Truth and open our minds and hearts to the *Spirit of Truth*. Only in the love of the Third Person can we see Love. We must yield our whole life to the Truth, the Truth that cannot be proved. God, Son of God, Holy Spirit: Three and One.

Have mercy upon me The prayer of the beggar; the prayer of the captive; the prayer of the dependant. *Have mercy* can only express an explicit acknowledgment of one not only subordinate to another but also, one acutely aware of his own peril at the hands of him whom he is beseeching for mercy. *Have mercy*: I deserve nothing in my own right. *Have mercy*: I know that in you alone lies salvation. Open my eyes. Raise me from my bed. Heal me from leprosy. I believe in your divine power. Christ God, have mercy.

A sinner I know that I am a sinner – a sinner above all. But Christ, my God, you ate with publicans and sinners. You came to call me to repentance, not the righteous. The thief will be with you this night in Paradise. I know that if I repent from my heart, you will forgive. From my heart, the prayer of the heart: Lord Jesus Christ, Son of God, have mercy upon me, a sinner.

Much has been written on the actual mechanics of saying the Jesus Prayer – the posture of the body, the breathing and so forth. But the Prayer is a personal prayer to a personal Saviour. Each one of us must choose his individual way. However, if we should wish to include the prayer into the very rhythm of our daily life, then it would seem appropriate to fit the prayer with the breath of life, breathing in, perhaps, with the opening words, 'Lord, Jesus Christ, Son of God', and breathing out with 'have mercy upon me a sinner'. But in no circumstances should this suggestion, or any other, be taken as a 'directive' to 'meditation'. The prayer is our weapon, our armour, for the daily battle in life against the evil in ourselves and against the wiles of the Devil. The prayer is *active* in its silence as no other.

How many times should we repeat it? There is no answer. We say it when and how we can. If we should wish to say the prayer at a particular time – for example, in the morning before we face the world, or at night before we sleep, it is better to start with a very few repetitions and then, perhaps, the prayer will gradually take over and we shall repeat it more freely. It may even continue in our hearts, through the rhythm of the working day and through the night.

I cannot overstress that the Jesus Prayer is not a means of leaving the world. It is rather a means, if it is a means, of uniting heaven and earth, of refusing to be absorbed in the world around and of consistently, whatever the circumstances, putting our purest attention on what is beyond the world. The prayer, as all Orthodox religious practice, is entirely *practical*: 'I am the vine, ye are the branches: he that abideth in me, and I in him, the same bringeth forth much fruit: for without me ye can do nothing.'

But perhaps the greatest joy of the Jesus Prayer for each of us is that it is entirely secret. No one should or does know when we pray it, how we pray it, and (if such a term can be applied) with what success.

The Jesus Prayer: the *secret* prayer of the heart – secret to man, open to God.

Chapter 7

Conclusion

In the presence of God there is no past and no future.

We have considered who we are as Orthodox: Christians who hold fast to the faith of our forefathers, who will not move from the Tradition as laid down by the Fathers of the Church in the Apostolic Tradition; Christians who believe in the Holy Spirit, ever and again, not as the One of the Trinity who inspires us consciously or unconsciously to make changes dictated by the fashions of the world, by what is considered 'politically correct', or 'equal rights'. The Martyrs of the Church had no equal rights, and they were martyred because they would not bow down to political or 'trendy' demands or be coaxed into putting the so-called happiness of their fellow creatures before the Divine Truth.

We have considered how, as Orthodox, we do not believe that we can add anything of our own to what was laid down once and for all by the apostles and the Fathers of the Seven Ecumenical Councils. We are content to pray what our forefathers prayed and we do not assume that we know the tenets of our faith any better than they did, because of our technical skill.

We think it more reasonable to teach our children the traditional liturgical language of our country rather than constantly having to re-write the liturgy to meet changes in language. In effect, we fight shy of 'fashion' in any form which it may take, in language or otherwise. It seems to us that *fashion*, as opposed to tradition, is *world* which our God told us directly to shun.

In the face of eternity, 'changes' directed by time or 'new' scholarship seem totally misplaced. Even if some

92

scholar does discover that a phrase in the Gospel has some previously hidden meaning, or another scholar proves that a manuscript or piece of manuscript is spurious, or yet another Gospel is dug up from under a crater, or that all St Paul's epistles are fakes – it can make no difference to our faith. Our faith is beyond human proof and outside immanent definition. Nothing can be adequate to the Divine Truth, so a few 'mistakes' mean nothing in the face of ultimate Truth. We do not believe in the incidental human attributes to our faith – we believe in what we can neither define nor prove. We cannot grasp the ultimate Truth, however precise or unreliable our information. We touch the hem of Christ's garment, but do not seek to analyse the thread of his cloak.

All is *Mystery*: if we wish to sum up the Orthodox attitude in the last count, that is perhaps the keyword. And we never forget that this *Mystery*, the *Divine Mystery*, for us is the greatest joy. If God were simply a superior human being, a type of Father Christmas, how boring the prospect of life eternal would be!

The key to the true Orthodox believer is ever and again the same key, the key which is the door to the sheepfold, the key which opens to us the ineffable joy of *not* knowing, but following blindly yet trustingly the voice of our Shepherd. Let us be educated, let us know every cog of the machine, every nuance of the atom, every square inch of the moon. And then let us stop. We *cannot* know what is beyond our human intellect.

There is a deep peace, a serenity, in being Orthodox; nothing is demanded of us. No proof. No justification. No learning. Just faith.

What is our last glimpse of Orthodoxy?

A *whirligig* of prayer; no single meditation; a whirlpool of experience: blessing, grief, joy. Earthquake: the Cross looming, angels in a blaze of

93

light, dazzling white garments, voices praising, voices blaspheming, voices mocking, voices lamenting. Beasts, birds, men, women, children: sick, cursing, praising. A riot of psalms, thunder of prophets. Little human sense. Divine meaning.

And what of death?

Generalizations are dangerous and tend to deviate from the truth but, bearing this in mind, it would seem that the Orthodox attitude to life and death differs somewhat in one particular from that of fellow Christians.

All Christians recognize the evil in the world. But, and here I *am* generalizing, the effect on us of this recognition is not uniform. The West turns to the world to teach, to reform, to heal. We turn away from the world and seek the wilderness for individual survival. Since we tend to divorce ourselves from earthly activity, and are inclined to escape spiritually if not in actual practice, death ceases to be a rude interruption to our activity. We may weep for those we love because we miss their presence, but consistently we live towards death.

Orthodox spirituality, if we allow ourselves to generalize in the broadest way, ultimately depends not on transforming this world but on looking beyond this world towards the life eternal. Christ blessed this division of human labour – some he kept as his disciples, some he sent home into the world.

The *objectivity* of the Orthodox attitude of faith allows no meditation to escape reality. This world is real. We know that, whatever else, we are finite creatures and that we cannot from our side attain to the divine. We cannot see God, the Trinity, yet we have seen God, Jesus Christ. We cannot know his will, yet we can follow his word. We cannot define God, yet we can wash his feet with our tears of repentance.

And, we rejoice. We rejoice that God is unattainable either by the critical working of our rational minds or by the flights of meditative prayer. God *is* God. We prostrate before him, finite creatures that we are:

Holy God
Holy Strong
Holy Deathless
Have mercy upon us.

A Glossary of Orthodox Terms

After-Supper Service The last service of the day, equivalent to Compline.

Antidoron Literally 'instead of the gift', this is bread, blessed but not consecrated in the preparation for the Eucharist, normally distributed to the faithful at the end of the Liturgy, to be consumed before any subsequent meal or kept for future consumption at home.

Antiphons Verses appointed to be sung in place of the Typika (Psalms 102 and 145, see *Typika*) and the Beatitudes at the Liturgy, normally at feasts; in common practice in Greek parishes they are sung on all Sundays.

Apolytikion (Tropar) The verses (short hymn) of the saint, or feast or other celebration of the day.

Aposticha Verses (*stichira*) sung at the end of Vespers and at the end of Matins when not a feast day.

Apostle The name commonly given to the appointed reading, at the Liturgy, from the Epistle of the day.

Beatitudes Sung in the Liturgy other than when Antiphons are appointed (see *Antiphons*). Verses appropriate to the day are inserted into the Beatitudes.

Behaviour (These are a few general hints that may be followed to avoid causing offence; more specific guidance is given elsewhere under various headings.)

On meeting a priest it is normal to ask for a blessing by placing one hand over the other in a cupping gesture, and kissing the priest's hand after the blessing is given. It is also usual to kiss the hand of an Abbot or Abbess on meeting; however, do not try to kiss priests, deacons, monks or nuns in general greeting, and when addressing them do not use their Christian name without the preceding title.

In church do not stand with your hands behind your back and if, for any reason, you need to sit during a service find a bench or chair, never sit on the floor. If you have children with you train them to stand quietly in front of you. Do not turn over pages in trying to follow the service; in fact books are not allowed in church for the congregation. A woman should never approach anything holy wearing lipstick and, as a rule, her head should always be covered in church.

Whatever you are doing stop and stand still during the Lord's Prayer, the Creed and the Gospel. Kneeling and full prostration (see *Prostration*) are not permitted on Sundays (see *Resurrection*) but, in practice, they are permitted at certain points of the Divine Liturgy.

Black and White Clergy   There are two orders of priests, 'black' (i.e. monks) and 'white' (i.e. married). In ordinary circumstances monk-priests do not serve parishes and they live in monasteries; the 'white' married priests serve parishes with their wives to help in parish duties. Monks are addressed as 'Father' followed by the monastic Christian name (never the surname); married priests simply as 'Father' (the Russian *batushka*).

Bright Week   (Week of Light) The week following Pascha (Easter); it is a week of no fasting, of joy and festivity and culminates in the Sunday dedicated to the Apostle Thomas.

Candles   Candles are lit in prayer, both at home and in church. Before going into church it is usual to buy candles for prayers to be offered for the living and the dead; they are lit in front of ikons of one's personal choice. At certain services candles are held, in prayer, by the faithful, e.g. the Panikhida (see *Panikhida*) at Pascha throughout the Resurrection service; at baptisms, weddings, funerals and in processions. During church services the bringing of a candle from, or placed before the altar signifies a solemn moment, e.g. the reading of the Gospel; the procession bearing the Holy Gifts; the Communion of the Priests. The candle frequently symbolizes the Word or presence of Christ.

Canons   1. The Ordinances of the Church devised in early years and preserved untouched by Tradition (see *Tradition* and *Economy*). 2. Liturgical poems, comprising nine odes based on the eight canticles of the Old Testament and the ninth of the Magnificat and Benedictus; sung principally at Matins, but also in the

After-Supper and Midnight Services and in special services.

Cathechumen One preparing for baptism into the Church; a baptized Christian, if he has been duly baptized in the name of the Trinity, is not regarded as a catechumen when preparing for reception into the Orthodox Church. In practice today no one is sent out of the Liturgy when the dismissal for the Catechumens is pronounced as sacrilegious behaviour is not anticipated.

Censing Censing occurs at fixed times during the services for blessing, cleansing and prayer; at home it is permissible to use incense in prayer but it is not essential. When a priest censes the congregation it is proper to bow one's head but not cross oneself (see *Sign of the Cross*). When the priest censes the ikons it is proper, if possible, to stand aside.

Confession Confession is obligatory before Holy Communion (see *Holy Communion*); in practice, owing to more frequent communicating, confession may not be demanded before every Communion, but, *in no circumstances* may Communion be made without the blessing of the officiating priest which should be sought *before* the service. Confession should normally be made to one's parish priest, or possibly to a spiritual father in a monastery. A life confession is sometimes appointed, as for example before reception into the Church, but normally confession only applies to what is immediately on one's conscience, i.e. actual thoughts and deeds. In the Orthodox Church, confession is seen as confession to Christ, *not* to the priest who is the witness; thus the one confessing does not face the priest, but stands at his side facing the Gospel and the Cross.

Creed (The) The Nicene Creed is used in the Liturgy, without the Filioque (and the Son).

Cross (The) (see *Sign of the Cross*). In Orthodox tradition each side of the crossbeam and the section above are of equal length; in the Russian tradition there are two further crosspieces, one horizontal near the top for the inscription and one oblique foot-rest.

Daily Prayer (see *Service Books*)   The day is divided into
services, the times varying according to sunset or to
local conditions. Ideally *all* the services are said in
churches and monasteries; in practice parishes vary
widely in what they can undertake, and large monasteries can manage more than small ones. In Orthodox
tradition no single person is bound to the daily office,
only the Church as a whole; what we cannot manage,
therefore, someone else is undertaking; this reminds us
that we are within the Communion of Saints. The day
begins with Vespers on the preceding evening; the
After-Supper Service introduces the silence of the
night; the Midnight Service is followed by Matins of
which Lauds forms a part, and the First Hour is
normally attached to Matins; the Third and Sixth
Hours are said in the morning; the Ninth Hour usually
precedes Vespers. On the eve of Sundays and Feasts it
is customary to have a Vigil Service, of varying length,
comprising, when celebrated in full, the Ninth Hour,
Great Vespers, After-Supper, Matins and the First
Hour. There are manuals in English which have
selected prayers out of the Service Books for daily use
at home, and on special occasions.

Deacon   An ordained rank in the Orthodox Church, not
necessarily a step to priesthood, but which has its own
duties. A deacon offers up the litanies in the Liturgy,
and reads the Gospel. When there is no deacon the
priest undertakes these duties as well as his own. A
deacon may be married or single.

Divine Liturgy (The)   The 'Mass' of the West. Liturgy is
not a term used for all services but kept strictly to the
one Service.

Economy   Permission granted for actions not strictly
allowed by the Canons of the Church (see *Canons*).
Economy in the Orthodox tradition emphasizes that
'*charity*' should be respected above any laws: however,
the practice of economy can be abused if it is merely to
satisfy a personal whim or indulgence.

Ekteneia   A Litany, or prayer of supplication, offered up
by the deacon, or by the priest if there is no deacon. The
choir, or people, respond with 'Lord have mercy' or
'Grant this, O Lord' as appropriate.

Ephraim (Ephrem) Prayer (The) See pp. 87–88. By tradition this is used by the faithful particularly in the Great Lent. *Note*: the prayer is not said on Sundays, even in the Great Lent, when prostrations are forbidden.

Exapostilarion A short hymn said or sung at the end of the canons in Matins as appointed for the day.

Fast (see also *Fasting*) Fast days are listed in the Church calendar. In brief: Wednesdays and Fridays throughout the year, except for special times of dispensation. In monasteries Mondays also may be a fast day. There are special single fast days, e.g. the Beheading of St John the Baptist. Fast days come before the great Feasts. *The Great Fast* comprises the forty days before Holy Week. Holy Week itself is the greatest fast of all. It is customary to abstain from all food on Holy Friday, or at any rate until the evening when the infirm or elderly may need refreshment.

Fasting Fasting is a traditional discipline of the Orthodox Church. The fundamental principle of fasting is to encourage a turning away from worldly pleasures to allow more serious concentration on Gospel teaching, thus fasting not only includes food but also the senses; weddings normally are not allowed at fasting times, particularly the Great Fast; entertainment, on the whole, should be avoided; above all, fasting should not involve the purchase of expensive 'fasting' food, or extra time spent on fasting recipes, nor should it be a matter of boasting. For an average person working in secular surroundings, in a non-Orthodox country, total fasting is hardly possible and it is better to settle on one 'kind' of fast and keep to it, rather than to attempt the impossible. A full fast means abstaining from meat, i.e. the meat itself, meat extracts, milk, eggs, cheese, butter, and whatever food includes these products. Fasting also implies that whatever is eaten should be simple, not highly spiced, without the accompaniment of alcohol, and one 'proper' meal should suffice, but again this is not a rule and depends on circumstances. Fasting, above all, should be accompanied by *prayer*, and is an *act of love* not a penance. On certain days of the year no fasting is permitted, e.g. at Pascha and the week following; at Christmas up to the Theophany (Epiphany).

Feasts   There are twelve Great Feasts in the year, specified in the Church calendar, and other feasts of varying significance, all having their individual characteristics in the services of their day. The twelve Great Feasts are:

1. The Nativity (Christmas) 25 Dec–7 Jan
2. The Theophany (Epiphany) 6–19 Jan
3. The Meeting of the Lord 2–15 Feb
4. The Annunciation 25 Mar–7 Apr
5. The Transfiguration 6–19 Aug
6. The Falling Asleep of the Mother of God 15–28 Aug
7. The Nativity of the Mother of God 8–21 Sept
8. Exaltation of the life-giving Cross 14–27 Sept
9. Entry of the Mother of God into the Temple 21 Nov–4 Dec
10. The Entry into Jerusalem of the Lord
11. Ascension
12. Pentecost (Holy Trinity)

Pascha (Easter) is the Feast of Feasts.

It is as improper not to feast at feast times as not to fast at fasting time; the Church makes it clear that not to rejoice is as much a heresy as not to mourn. But, of course, this does not mean that feasting is an excuse for licence and gluttony.

Flowers   Flower arrangements are not part of the Orthodox tradition; in no circumstances should flowers be put on the Holy Table, and artificial flowers in church are out of the question. It is permissible to decorate the church with cut flowers, particularly at Easter, or to put containers with flowers in them on the floor beneath ikons, but not as carefully arranged ornamentation in their own right.

Forgiveness (Cheese) Sunday   The last Sunday before the Great Fast. It is customary for the faithful after Vespers to ask forgiveness of each other before entering into the Fast. No meat is eaten in the week following, only cheese.

Gospel (The)   The Gospel refers both to the book containing the Gospels and also to the appointed reading from the Gospel in the Liturgy or other service. The New Testament, for general use, contains the Gospels and Epistles and is not normally bound with the Old Testament (Bible); for use in church the Gospel and the Apostle are usually bound separately.

Graces   At a common meal no one should begin eating before the blessing. On one's own it is customary to cross oneself before and after eating or drinking. The Lord's Prayer is frequently used as the grace before a meal and a common after meal grace is: 'We thank thee, O Christ our God, that thou hast satisfied us with thy earthly blessings; deprive us not of thy heavenly Kingdom; but, as thou camest in the midst of thy disciples, O Saviour, and gavest them peace, so come to us and save us.'

Holy Communion   The Eucharist, the central point of the Liturgy. Holy Communion should only be taken by the faithful who have made their confession (see *Confession*), or at least asked a blessing before the service. In Orthodox practice the bread consecrated for Communion must be leavened (see *Prosfora*) and the wine red, made from grapes. The faithful make their communion in both kinds, the particles of bread dipped in the wine and administered on a spoon. After communicating it is customary to drink some blessed wine and eat a piece of blessed bread as a means of purifying. After partaking of Holy Communion the communicant should not kiss a priest's hand, nor venerate ikons, nor kneel, nor prostrate, for the rest of the day.

Holy Oil   Oil blessed and kept for the anointing of the sick, or dying. An anointing with holy oil has always the element of healing and is used on other occasions, as for example the reception of a convert.

Holy Mountain (The)   Mount Athos in Greece, the site of ancient monasteries living in the unbroken tradition of the Orthodox Church.

Holy Table (The)   The altar in the sanctuary.

Holy Water   Blessed water: from the *Blessing of the Waters* on the Theophany (Epiphany). Holy water is used for health and cleansing, e.g. when blessing a house.

Idiorhythmic   (see *Monasteries*).

Ikons   An ikon is *not* an ikon unless it is painted in the true tradition, according to traditional rules. Once it is painted it should be blessed, either by a full or partial service. Sometimes an ikon is blessed by being laid on the Holy Table. Whatever the method, an ikon has a sacramental nature and purpose not to be confused with religious drawings. By economy (see *Economy*) paper ikons are now in use, but there is *no* economy for ikons painted idiosyncratically outside the tradition, nor for an indiscriminate use of the term. It is customary to bow before an ikon, to cross oneself and kiss the ikon at the base. *Never* handle an ikon or put one's palm over it, or place a finger on it. To carry an ikon wrap it carefully in a clean white cloth. To carry more than one ikon place the ikons facing each other.

Ikonostasis   The high screen with ikons on it, dividing the altar (Sanctuary) from the main body of the church. Only priests may open and pass through the central Royal Doors in it; there are also doors at either end of the ikonostasis, North and South.

Intercession   All the litanies include intercessions; a priest may be asked to offer up particular names of those sick, in distress, or to remember the dead by name. It is customary before a Liturgy for prosfora (see *Prosfora*) to be made available for the faithful to buy; the faithful will then write a list for the living, putting their own names first, with one prosfora, and a list of the dead with a second prosfora; Christian names only should be written on the lists. The prosfora, together with the lists, should be handed in to the priest before the service; after the fragments have been cut out the prosforas are returned to the faithful for consumption. Sometimes a large prosfora is baked and presented on behalf of a member of a particular family. If for some reason there is no prosfora available, a list of names (one for the living, one for the dead) can still be handed in.

Jesus Prayer (The)   The prayer of the heart, practised by Orthodox Christians at all times and in all places; the words may be said in full or in part: 'Lord Jesus Christ, Son of God, have mercy upon me, a sinner.' The Jesus Prayer is a secret, unceasing, inner prayer, and traditionally is not said aloud with other people. The prayer-cord (see *Prayer-cord*) is frequently used in conjunction with the prayer. See pp. 88–91.

Kneeling   Kneeling in the Orthodox tradition is not permitted on Sundays or during the Paschal period; however, it is not unusual for the faithful to kneel on Sundays for the Lord's Prayer and to prostrate during the prayers of consecration and before the chalice. There must be no kneeling after Holy Communion. Vespers on the evening of Pentecost is frequently called 'kneeling Vespers' since kneeling and prostration begin again after the Paschal season.

Kolyva (Greek) (Russian: *Kutia*)   Wheat, or rice, mixed with honey and raisins, or sultanas, or apples, eaten at panikhidas (see *Panikhida*).

Kontakion (Greek) (Russian: *Kondak*)   A short hymn appointed for the day, said or sung at the appropriate points in the services.

Kulitch (Russian)   A tall bun-cake, made with many eggs, flavoured with saffron and eaten at Pascha.

Lauds   This is not a separate service but constitutes the end of Matins.

Lity   The ceremony of the litany of fervent supplication appointed for the greater feasts when the blessing of the bread is celebrated; the Lity precedes the Aposticha in Great Vespers (see *Aposticha*).

Lord's Prayer (The)   The doxology at the end of the Lord's Prayer is not said by the people. It is customary to stand still whenever the Lord's Prayer is said in church, or to kneel; one should never sit or allow children to run about while the prayer is being said; it should always be remembered that this is *the Lord's* prayer.

Matins   Constitutes the second service of the day, following the Midnight Service. Matins is normally said early in the morning in monasteries. In Greek parishes it may precede the Liturgy, and at Vigils it is said at night following the services appointed to precede it.

Meat Week   The penultimate week before the Great Fast; meat is eaten for the last time as in the final week only cheese is permitted.

Monasteries   A monastery is autonomous in so far that there are no 'orders' as in the Western tradition, and every monastery has its own *typikon* (rule). But, broadly speaking, the rules are very much the same, as all monasteries follow a similar tradition, suggested by St Basil, of monks (or nuns) living by their own labour, having no private property, going out only for necessity, saying the services and eating at a common table. There are *idiorhythmic* monasteries where monks or nuns retain their property, eat separately, even retain servants, but these are not in the main line of tradition. *Sketes* normally comprise a few monks or nuns gathered round a spiritual father or mother; the life can tend to be more ascetic, or intellectual, according to the nature of the *skete*, and the Jesus Prayer may replace the usual monastic services to a lesser or greater extent. Mixed monasteries are strictly forbidden, but traditionally a female monastery may be situated in the locality of a male monastery so as to benefit from the official visits of a priest-monk, or to receive some assistance with heavy manual work.

Mysteries   The Sacraments of the West are normally termed the Mysteries in the Orthodox Church, and there is no fixed number. Other than in this strictly sacramental sense, the Orthodox Church tends to avoid definition of what is beyond human understanding and prefers to rely on the concept of 'Mystery'.

Name Day   At baptism an Orthodox baby is given only one name which must be a recognized one in the list of saints; the saint's day is the name-day of the one baptized and is celebrated annually; in Russia, for example, the name-day was a more festive occasion than the birthday. Sometimes the saint chosen for the child was the one whose day fell nearest to the birthday. Converts, if their own names are not those of a listed saint, are given a new name on being received into the Orthodox Church.

Orthodoxy   The right or true belief, based on the decrees of the Seven Ecumenical Councils from the teaching of the Apostles, derived from Christ God (see *Tradition*).

Panikhida   Memorial service for the dead, celebrated on the third, ninth and fortieth days after death; and subsequently on birthdays or name-days, and on the anniversary of the death. A general panikhida, for all our forebears, is sung on special days of the year, e.g. the Saturday before the Great Fast begins. Saturdays throughout the year are days for remembrance of the dead.

Pascha   Easter: the Sunday of Resurrection. Pascha is regarded as the *Feast of Feasts*. N.B. the greeting of three kisses is a *Paschal* greeting; there is no tradition for prolonging it throughout the year. Pascha is also the name given in Russia to the festive cheese-cake eaten together with *kulitch* (see *Kulitch*).

Patriarch   The Patriarch is the Senior Bishop of an ecclesiastical jurisdiction: the Patriarch of Constantinople, although he has no additional power, is traditionally regarded as the first among equals. His patriarchate, as well as being local, extends over all Orthodox not living in an Orthodox country. It is the privilege of some monasteries to be *stavropegic*, i.e. to be responsible directly to the Patriarch of the jurisdiction and not to the local Bishop.

Podvig   A Russian word signifying an ascetic endeavour, or particular work under obedience.

Polyeleos   1. (Greek: 'much merciful') Psalms 134 and 135 sung at Matins on feasts and certain saints' days and Sundays. In Greek use, Psalm 44 is added on the feasts of the Mother of God.
2. (Greek: 'much oil') This is the name given to the big central lamp in church, lit at certain times of particular solemnity.

Prayer-cord   Beads, wooden or thick thread, strung together and normally numbering one hundred; used in silent praying of the Jesus Prayer (see *Jesus Prayer*).

Priest   A priest may only be recognized as the representative of the Bishop if he has been duly ordained by the laying on of hands, in the unbroken Apostolic line. A priest, normally, should not officiate outside his own parish without the permission of his Bishop, or in another diocese without the permission of the Bishop of that diocese (see *Black and White Clergy*).

Prokeimenon   Verses sung before the Apostle (see *Apostle*) in the Liturgy; before the Gospel in Matins; and daily in Vespers.

Prosfora (see *Intercession*) Small loaves used in the Proskomidi from which some particles are consecrated for the Eucharist and others are retained for intercession.

Proskomidi The preparation of the bread and wine before the Liturgy. The bread and wine are brought in for consecration at the Great Entrance to the accompaniment of the Cherubic Hymn.

Prostration 1. Crossing and bowing, the fingers of the right hand touching the ground. This is called the small prostration.

2. A full bow, i.e. the body prostrated with the forehead touching the ground.

Rason / Rasofor The *rason* is the monastic garment; the bestowing of the rason is the ceremony of the blessing of a *rasofor* (novice).

Royal Doors The doors in the centre of the Ikonostasis (see *Ikonostasis*), dividing the altar (Sanctuary) from the main body of the church.

Royal Hours Possibly so called because these are the daily hours expanded wth readings, Apostle, and Gospel, for solemn occasions, and may have been given the name first in Constantinople when attended by the Emperor; the Royal Hours are said on Holy Friday when no Liturgy is permitted and on the Eve of Christmas and Theophany (Epiphany).

Resurrection The term applies not only to Pascha but to all Sundays; thus, for example the particular hymn (*Apolytikion*) for Sunday will be referred to as the Apolytikion of the Resurrection.

Saints Every saint in the Orthodox Church has a day of commemoration; the saints have their degrees of celebration, some only, for example, with three verses in Vespers, some sharing a common Apolytikion (see *Apolytikion*), others with an Apolytikion of their own, some with a Great Doxology in Matins and others with a full Vigil. The details are given in the Typikon (see *Service Books*) of the day. It is customary to be named after a saint and to have a special veneration for that saint. Most saints, if not all, have traditional personal ikons. There are saints venerated throughout the Orthodox world, others are more local, and some are totally local. The consecration of a saint is normally by public veneration and some form of manifestation from the saint; for example, a body incorrupt, or miracles at the tomb.

Septuagint The Greek translation from the Hebrew of the Bible approximately in the third century BC; there are certain differences from the Hebrew Bible as we have it today, such as the numbering of the Psalms. The Septuagint version of the Bible is used by the Orthodox Church.

Service Books (see also *Daily Prayer*). The Orthodox Church has no equivalent of the Roman Breviary or Anglican Book of Common Prayer, but retains all the Books unabbreviated; this means that every service has its 'skeleton' of fixed parts, with the movable parts introduced according to the day, month, season; this means the retention of all the books necessary for each 'movable' part.

1. *Euchologion* (Russian: *Trebnik*): comprehensive book of all the priest's needs.

2. *Horologion* (Russian: *Molitvoslov*): this contains all the fixed parts of the daily services, together with a calendar of the saints and feasts, and the Apolytikion (see *Apolytikion*) and Kontakion (see *Kontakion*) of the day.

3. *Ieratikon* (Russian: *Sluzhebnik*): the priest's 'parts' in the Church services.

4. *Irmologions*: contains every *Irmos* to be sung at the opening of the Odes in the Matins Canons; the Irmologion will also give the Katavasia (sung at the end of the Odes) of the day.

5. *Menaion* (in twelve monthly parts): the monthly cycle of services; saints and feasts for each day of the month.

6. *Paraklitiki* (Russian: *Oktoichos*): the services of the weekly cycle of eight tones, each day of each week in the tone of the week. There are eight musical tones which follow each other week by week, beginning with Tone I on the Sunday of holy Apostle Thomas (the Sunday after Pascha).

7. *Pentikostarion*: this replaces the Paraklitiki, for every day from Pascha to All Saints (the Sunday after Pentecost).

8. *Triodion*: replaces the Paraklitiki, except on Saturdays and Sundays, throughout the Great Fast and Holy Week. The Triodion comes into use four Sundays before the Great Fast.

9. *The Typikon*: this gives the directions for combining all the above Service Books (see *Typikon*).

Sign of the Cross The fourth and fifth fingers should be placed in the palm of the right hand (representing the two persons, divine and human, of Christ) and the first two fingers and thumb should touch each other (representing the Holy Trinity). Crossing should not be hasty but, with the fingers in the correct position, first the forehead, then the breast, then the right shoulder and then the left shoulder should be touched, with due thought. The purposes of crossing oneself are varied but principally:

a) To affirm one's faith. To show one's collaboration in any point of a Church Service, or for emphasis and punctuation in one's own prayers.

b) As a protection against evil.

c) As a general reminder to oneself of one's Christian profession.

d) As a silent prayer or intention of memory.

Skete (see *Monasteries*)

Staretz An elder, a spiritual father. A staretz is not appointed, either by others or by himself, but he just 'happens' by people finding him out and seeking his help. The tradition of staretzi flourished in Russia and Dostoevsky gives a memorable picture of a staretz in Fr. Zossima (*The Brothers Karamazov*).

Theotokion Any verses addressed to the Mother of God; on fast days the Theotokion is replaced by the *Stavrotheotokion*, i.e. the theotokion of the Cross.

Theotokos Literally 'birth-giver of God', normally translated Mother of God.

Tones (see *Service Books*) In Slavonic usage they are numbered 1–8, but in Greek 1–4 and then: Plagial 1, Plagial 2, Grave, Plagial 4.

Tradition The Tradition of the Church is the Orthodoxy,

the right belief, carefully preserved and handed down throughout the centuries, from the first Apostles, through the Fathers and the Councils, to the present day. We believe that the Holy Spirit inspires and keeps alive this living Tradition of the Incarnate Word of God. Tradition, in this true sense, should not be confused with *tradition*, that is, national customs which have grown up in various Orthodox countries and which are loved by the people; there is no harm in local tradition provided it does not turn into superstition, is not exclusive, and does not assume the status of Tradition.

Trisagion   The Thrice-Holy, sung or read on many occasions: 'Holy God, Holy Strong (Mighty), Holy Deathless (Immortal), have mercy upon us.'

Troparion (Tropar)   A verse, or verses.

Typika   In 'type', representing the Liturgy, sung after the ninth hour when there is no Liturgy. The Typika Psalms are sung normally at the Liturgy preceding the Beatitudes.

Typikon   The typikon is the name given to the particular rule of a monastery (see also *Service Books*).

Week (*days of*)   All the days of the week have a special significance:

Monday The Angels

Tuesday St John the Baptist, the Forerunner

Wednesday The Betrayal (Services of the Cross as Friday)

Thursday The Apostles and St Nicholas

Friday The Crucifixion

Saturday The Dead

Every day has its own Apolytikion and Kontakion and these are used if no special ones are appointed.

Sunday is set apart for the Resurrection.

Xirophagia   The eating of dry food in fast time (Gk.)

Yearly Cycle (see *Feasts, Fasts, Service Books*)   There is not a day in the year which has not a place in the worship of the Church.

Further Reading

Orthodox Spirituality, by A Monk of the Eastern Church, Third Edition, St Vladimir's Seminary Press, Crestwood, New York 10707, 1987.

The Orthodox Church, Kallistos Ware, Penguin, 1993.

The Religion of the Russian People, Pierre Pascal, St Vladimir's Seminary Press, 1989.

Mysticism and the Eastern Church, Nicholas Arseniev, St Vladimir's Seminary Press, 1984.

Eastern Christendom, Nicholas Zernov, Weidenfeld & Nicolson.

The Mystical Theology of the Eastern Church, Vladimir Lossky, James Clarke, 1957.